HENRY'S
DEMONS

ALSO BY PATRICK COCKBURN

Muqtada al-Sadr and the Battle for the Future of Iraq

The Occupation: War and Resistance in Iraq

The Broken Boy

Out of the Ashes: The Resurrection of Saddam Hussein
(with Andrew Cockburn)

HENRY'S DEMONS

LIVING WITH SCHIZOPHRENIA:
A FATHER AND SON'S STORY

Patrick and Henry Cockburn

SIMON &
SCHUSTER

London · New York · Sydney · Toronto

A CBS COMPANY

First published in Great Britain in 2011 by Simon & Schuster UK Ltd
A CBS

Copyright © 2011 by Patrick Cockburn and Henry Cockburn

This book is copyright under the Berne Convention.
No reproduction without permission.
All rights reserved.

The rights of Patrick Cockburn and Henry Cockburn to be identified as the authors
of this work have been asserted by them in accordance with sections 77 and 78
of the Copyright, Designs and Patents Act, 1988.

1 3 5 7 9 10 8 6 4 2

Simon & Schuster UK Ltd
1st Floor
222 Gray's Inn Road
London
WC1X 8HB

www.simonandschuster.co.uk

Simon & Schuster Australia
Sydney

A CIP catalogue copy for this book is available
from the British Library.

ISBN: 978-1-84737-703-6 (hardback)
978-0-85720-186-7 (trade paperback)

Printed in the UK by CPI Mackays, Chatham ME5 8TD

FOR JAN AND ALEX

HENRY'S
DEMONS

Timeline of Henry's Hospital Stays

February 6, 2002: Henry is rescued from sea of Newhaven and taken to the hospital.

February–April 2002: The Priory Hospital.

April–October 2002: Home in Canterbury.

October–December 2002: Henry returns to Brighton University and finishes the term.

January–June 2003: Anselm ward, St Martin's Hospital, Canterbury.

June–August 2003: "The Grove" Rehabilitation Centre, Ramsgate.

September 2003: Anselm ward, St Martin's Hospital.

October–December 2003: Amber ward (unlocked, for less ill patients), St Martin's Hospital.

January 2004: Rehabilitation centre in Ethelbert Road, Canterbury.

February 2004 (very briefly): Amber ward, St Martin's Hospital.

February–May 2004: Anselm ward, St Martin's Hospital.

May 2004–May 2006: Dudley Venables House or DVH (the "secure" ward), St Martin's Hospital.

May 2006–January 2007: Bethlem Royal Hospital, Bromley, south London.

January 2007–October 2009: Cygnet Hospital, Beckton, east London.

October 2009–present: Cygnet Lodge, a "step-down" facility or halfway house, Lewisham, south-east London.

PREFACE

This book is about how my son Henry was diagnosed with schizo-phrenia in 2002 and how this affected him and our family. As he started to recover – and this recovery is by no means complete – about three years ago, I began to think that he and I should write about our experiences. I felt that we might turn everything he had suffered into an asset. He was ideally placed to write from the *inside* about what it was like to have an acute mental illness in which trees and bushes spoke and voices called him to flee into the night or plunge into icy water where he might drown. He knew what it was like to live in men-tal hospitals, places that most people regard with ignorance and dread. I believed that Henry and I could serve a broader public purpose by making schizophrenia and mental illness in general less of a mystery which people are embarrassed to discuss. I began to think with grow-ing enthusiasm about writing a book with Henry about what he, along with the rest of his family, had been through.

The more I considered it, the more I thought that what was really needed was a book that would be not only different from others but unique in its description of mental illness. It would definitely not be just a book with a joint byline, which in fact would be an account by me of Henry's ordeal, like the best-selling but ghostwritten memoirs of so many sportsmen, generals, and politicians. I believed this would not do, even if I faithfully tried to report everything which had happened to my son. The mental world in which he had been living was so different from my own that his firsthand testimony alone could convey what it is like to hear voices and see visions, to be tormented by waves of unexplained guilt and to lose all sense of the difference between what is imaginary and what is real. Only Henry himself could describe the landscape of this hidden planet on which he lived, along with so many others suffering from schizophrenia.

I ran my idea for the book past him, and he liked it, though when we spoke of his hallucinations, he objected to the word, since to him they remain genuine events. I thought the way he defended the reality of his experiences would be an advantage because, though people with mental disorders have written books, they commonly do so after they are largely recovered. This is not good enough; I know, having reported many wars, how difficult it is to recapture intense emotions like fear of death even seconds after the reason for one's terror has disappeared. I remembered the question asked by Alexander Solzhenitsyn in *One Day in the Life of Ivan Denisovitch:* "Can a man who is warm understand a man who is freezing?" I do not believe that somebody who does not have schizophrenia, or has recovered from it, can fully understand and describe what it is like for somebody who still has it. Henry can do so because he is well enough to write but not so distant from his psychosis that it has become ancient history in his own mind.

I worried about subjecting Henry to extra stress by asking him to write about what had happened to him. I knew he could recall in detail all that had occurred because he told me that, surprisingly, his memory had improved during his years in the hospital. At first I was incredulous, but when I tested him with a few questions, I found he was right – he could remember the names of people whom he had met fleetingly five years earlier. I had not expected this because I had read somewhere that the memory of people with schizophrenia gets poorer, not better. I knew Henry could write fluently, as he was highly educated and had done well on school exams, though these were often preceded by spasms of doubt about his own abilities. This lack of self-confidence persisted. It took a lot of coaxing and encouragement to get him to write, but once he did, his style had a sort of radiant simplicity and truthfulness about his actions. What he wrote was also full of surprises for me, though I thought I knew him so well, showing that only somebody suffering from this strange and terrible illness can describe what it is really like.

What follows is our story of living with schizophrenia.

Patrick Cockburn
Canterbury, March 2010

CHAPTER ONE
Patrick

On February 8, 2002, I called my wife, Jan, by satellite phone from Kabul, where I was writing about the fall of the Taliban. It had been snowing, and as I leaned out of the window of the guesthouse where I was staying to get better reception, I felt very cold. Jan's voice sounded thin and distant but more anxious than I had ever heard it, and I felt a sense of instant dread as I realised there had been some disaster. I could not make out the details, but I grasped that Henry, our twenty-year-old son, had nearly died when he swam Newhaven estuary fully clothed and was rescued by fishermen as he left the near-freezing water. The fishermen feared he might be suffering from hypothermia and took him to a general hospital in Brighton. The police had been called, they had decided that Henry was a danger to himself, and he was now in a mental hospital. Jan gave me the phone number, and as soon as I had finished speaking to her, I tried to call the hospital. After many failures on the satellite phone, I got through and explained who I was. A nurse said that Henry was all right, and I asked to speak to him. When he got on the phone, he said, "I'm okay, Dad," in a weak and frightened voice that did not reassure me. I replied, with an assumed confidence I certainly did not feel, that he should not worry because everything would turn out all right in the end.

I had told Jan I would rush home as quickly as I could. Kabul was then the worst place in the world from which to leave swiftly in an emergency. The only way of getting a flight out of the city was to fly on a United Nations or foreign aid organization plane from Bagram airport, north of Kabul. But I knew these flights were infrequent and often refused to carry journalists. I had recent experience of the land routes out of Afghanistan, and all were highly dangerous. I decided the only way to get home quickly was to drive east to Islamabad in Pakistan and take a plane from there. I explained my plan to my driver, Gul Agha, who gulped a little at the thought of going through the Kabul Gorge to Jalalabad and the Pakistan border because roving bands of Taliban were still attacking travellers on the road. They had executed four journalists in a convoy that had stopped at one of their checkpoints. I told Gul that my eldest son was very ill, and he said that, if such was the case, he would simply drive over anybody who tried to stop us. In any event, the road was mostly empty. There were few other vehicles or gunmen manning checkpoints, and I thought that the bandits or Taliban fighters must have become discouraged by the cold and the lack of travellers to rob, and gone home. We reached the Khyber Pass and the Pakistani border, where officials issued me a transit visa, and leaving Gul Agha behind in Afghanistan, I took another car to Peshawar, where I spent the night. The following morning I drove to Islamabad and got a plane back to England.

There was probably something expiatory in this mad dash. As I sat in the back of Gul's car, I wondered what I had been doing talking to Afghan warlords and drug smugglers when my own son was in such trouble. I was completely shocked and taken by surprise at what had happened to Henry. In late January, Jan had mentioned on the phone what we later realised were some warning signs, such as Henry going barefoot, being stopped by the police when he climbed up a viaduct wall, and his suspicion of mechanical objects such as clocks. At the time I did not quite know what to make of this behaviour, but I was perplexed rather than deeply worried because I suspected that eccentricity on Henry's part had been misinterpreted. It never occurred to me that these might be dangerous signs of a mental disorder, since I knew nothing about mental illness. When I had last seen Henry at Christmas six weeks earlier in our house in Ardmore in Ireland, he had seemed to me to be his usual intelligent, charming, and humorous self.

Ever since he was a child, Henry was intensely alive and interested in everything and everybody around him. He had elfinlike good looks, with curly light brown hair, sparkling grey-green eyes, an impish smile, and great warmth. Over the years I had become used to reading reports from Henry's teachers praising him enthusiastically for being able, original, likeable, and articulate, but often adding, with varying degrees of frustration, that he could be spectacularly ill organised, was forgetful of all rules and regulations, and did only what he wanted to do himself. This praise and criticism of Henry was consistent over the years, from infants' school in Moscow in 1985 when he was three to his public school in Canterbury when he was eighteen. He was naturally rebellious, but his rebellion took the form of evading the rules rather than confrontation. There was a certain quirkiness in his nature. He found King's School in Canterbury, an ancient foundation beside the cathedral, too snobbish, so, to meet more ordinary townspeople, he started to juggle coloured balls in the streets while a friend stood beside him playing the violin. From an early age, his artistic talent was apparent. His paintings and sketches were strikingly elegant and original, winning him at least one valuable prize. For all his messiness and disorganisation, he could work very hard when he had to and had no difficulty getting the right A-levels to enter art college in Brighton at the end of 2001.

Henry and Patrick at a party in 2000

Henry and I had always been very close, and as he entered the final years of his education, I was pleased that his early life appeared to have been happy and untroubled. He was invariably high-spirited and good company. In the back of my mind, I was glad his childhood had not been torpedoed by any disaster, which was what had happened at least in part to my own when I caught polio in Ireland at the age of six in 1956. After a nasty time in the hospital, I had, for several years, worn a plastic waistcoat to keep my spine straight and used a wheelchair to get around before graduating to crutches. I threw these away at the age of ten, but I have always had a severe limp, cannot run, and do not drive. As I watched Henry growing up, I felt all the closer to him because the evident happiness of his childhood seemed to compensate for the occasional misery of my own. As he grew older, I was proud of the way he got on well with my friends, mostly foreign correspondents, though they were far older than he was. Very occasionally, I worried about the lack of friction between Henry and me, thinking it might be a sign of a lack of maturity on his part that his sense of identity was not developing a hard edge. He was not emotionally tough; he was too reliant on an easy social manner and too easily cast down by small setbacks in his life or occasional rejection by other people. I wondered if he might be something of a Peter Pan, a boy whose magical charm made it difficult for him to grow up.

Just before Jan rang me in Kabul to say that Henry had almost drowned, I had been far more concerned about Henry's thirteen-year-old brother, Alex. He was having a difficult time at King's, where he was in his second year as the top scholar. He had always been shy and more introverted than Henry, his smile gentle rather than impish. He read more, studied harder, and in a quiet way, was highly competitive. He always did well at school and was spectacularly good at mathematics, passing exams years before he was supposed to take them. I would find pieces of paper in the house in Canterbury covered with his abstruse mathematical calculations. He had a shock of dark hair, grey eyes, and a look of studiousness emphasised by a pair of black-framed spectacles, which made him look, as a young teenager, like the film version of Harry Potter. French schoolchildren, who often came to Canterbury to see the cathedral, would point excitedly at him in the street and shout: "'Arry Pottayr! 'Arry Pottayr!" A year earlier, when Henry was at art college in Brighton, Alex had won a valuable scholarship offered by King's, which cut his fees in half, and I had hoped this would boost his self-confidence. Unfortunately, it had exactly the opposite effect; during his first year, Alex felt that as the top scholar of his year, he was not living up to his own or others' expectations, and this depressed him. He had many friends at his previous school, but he was not making many new ones at King's. Some months earlier, when I was in Afghanistan covering the start of the war to over-throw the Taliban after 9/11, Jan had told me that Alex was very unhappy at school. I came back for his half term, travelling through the Hindu Kush mountains with some difficulty, but it was not clear what we could do about his distress. I said to Jan that it was unclear how to help Alex, but it was a relief that Henry's life seemed to be coming right at his art college. When I saw Henry at Christmas, I asked him how he was enjoying being a student in Brighton, and he said: "I have never been happier in my life."

I slept most of the way on the flight from Islamabad to England. I had prearranged a car to take me from the airport to Canterbury. Jan had lived in the ancient cathedral city for over twenty years in a little seventeenth-century house on Castle Street, opposite a park filled with lime trees that had pale green leaves. At one end of the street were the battered remains of a Norman castle which gave it its name, and looking down the street in the other direction, one could see the great tower of Canterbury Cathedral rising above the rooftops. The street itself had once been full of ordinary shops such as a watch mender and a greengrocer, but at the time of my return from Kabul, a housing boom had led to almost all these being replaced by estate agencies, the windows of which were filled with depressing pictures of ugly houses at high prices.

I had disliked the house for years because it was too small for me, though Jan, Henry, and Alex just fitted into it and were happy there during the years when the boys were growing up. As they loved the house, and I spent so much of my time living in houses or apartments of my own in other countries, I never felt I could insist on selling it

and buying a bigger one. This was symptomatic of Jan and my relationship: very affectionate but bearing the marks of long separations.
Jan and I had lived apart for extended periods since we first met, when
we were both students at Oxford in 1970. I had then gone to Belfast to
write my Ph.D. at the height of the Troubles, and while there, I had
decided to become a journalist rather than an academic. My father,
Claud, and my two elder brothers, Alexander and Andrew, were all
journalists so it seemed a natural thing to do. During the following
twenty-five years, I covered crises, rebellions, and wars everywhere
from Haiti to Afghanistan, working first for *The Financial Times* and
later for *The Independent*. I had been stationed as a correspondent
in Beirut, Moscow, Baghdad, Washington, and Jerusalem, as well as
living out of a suitcase for long periods in places such as Port-au-
Prince, Tehran, Kabul, and Chechnya. All this while Jan stayed in
academia, teaching English literature briefly at Liverpool University
and then for many years at the University of Kent at Canterbury.
My job was highly mobile and hers was largely stationary, though
she did manage two years in Moscow and also in Washington. Ours
was a marriage which seemed to work, though too many of our
communications were shouted messages over decrepit and antique
telephone lines from Beirut or by a satellite phone powered by a car
battery from villages in northern Afghanistan. Sitting in the back of
the hired car as I was driven from the airport to Canterbury that chill
February evening, I wondered if having his parents living in two different countries had contributed to Henry's breakdown.

I was not sure what this breakdown amounted to or how permanent
it would be, and when I saw Jan's slim shape outlined by the light
as she stood in the doorway of her house, I felt relieved that I could

learn the seriousness of what had happened to Henry. Even though on one level, I knew he had suffered a disaster and come near dying, I thought instinctively of mental illness as if it were a physical ailment, albeit a very serious one like a brain tumour, which might be dangerous but was also curable. After a quick embrace, I walked into the downstairs sitting room of Jan's house, which was dominated by an ancient brick fireplace to one side of which was a small red sofa. We sat on it together as Jan described the sinister changes she had seen in Henry since Christmas. It was, she said, as if another personality had been invading his mind and taking him over. Only then did I get an inkling of the depth of his psychosis. As she spoke, I began to see that our son was entering a different, nightmarish world induced by a mental disorder, though I did not yet really know what this implied or whether it was permanent. Jan knew a little more about mental illness than I did because there were signs of it in her family. Her grandmother had suffered from bipolar disorder and had been in and out of mental hospitals. Jan had also received sage advice about what Henry's symptoms might mean from her therapist, whom she had started seeing eighteen months earlier, when she was suffering from a severe depression brought on by a series of family deaths and disasters.

"It was not one single thing that Henry did which was so worrying in the days before he almost drowned at Newhaven," explained Jan on the night of my return. "It was rather an accumulation of many small but bizarre things that he did and said." Jan has a photographic memory, better than that of anybody I have ever known; she is able to recall pages of poetry she has read only a few times. She could remember in great detail all of Henry's actions since I had last seen him. Somewhere in the back of my mind, I was still hoping that at least some of Henry's actions could be explained by student eccentricity or his original cast of mind, but as Jan spoke, these hopes evaporated. The first incident had happened two weeks earlier, on January 28, when Henry had been arrested by the police and spent some hours in a cell. Passers-by had seen him, barefoot and dishevelled, climbing the dangerously high wall of a railway viaduct and reported him as a potential suicide. He stoutly denied to the police that he was trying to kill himself, claiming that he had climbed the viaduct to get a better view of Brighton. Henry, as we were to find over the coming years, could often sound convincing when explaining his most bizarre behaviour, and the police had let him go.

Henry's explanation of the viaduct incident might have been true, but Jan was worried enough to go to see him for lunch in Brighton the next weekend, taking Alex with her. The two brothers had always got on very well. The plan was that Alex would stay the night in Henry's room, which was in an apartment he shared with other art students in the Phoenix hall of residence in Brighton. The visit rapidly turned into a disaster. Jan and Alex drove down from Canterbury, arriving at the Phoenix at one P.M. on Saturday, expecting to meet Henry and go out to lunch. He was not there, though the door of his room was open, so they went in. The place was an appalling mess even by adolescent standards, with empty coffee cups, discarded takeaway meals, and dirty clothes all over the floor. On a table was a new-looking Indian book on teaching oneself meditation. A large cartoon-cum-doodle daubed on the wall looked half-finished, as if inspiration had run out before it was completed. Henry's mobile phone was lying on a desk, but it had been taken apart. Alex pointed out to Jan that Henry had taken the SIM card out so as to make absolutely sure it did not work. Jan noticed a strange object hanging out of the window: it turned out to be a plastic bucket full of rubbish attached by a string. Jan and Alex waited for three and a half hours in a state of increasing anger, but there was no sign of Henry. Jan was phoning the police to report him as a missing person when he finally turned up. He said unapologetically that he was so late because he had been "lost in town," though this seemed strange, as he had been living in Brighton since the previous October.

"Why did you ask Alex and me to lunch and then stand us up?" asked Jan, who was relieved to see him but at the same time furious.

"I'll make you lunch right now," Henry replied.

Jan told him they'd had a snack while they waited, and a shouting match followed. She saw that this was upsetting Alex, who was in a fragile emotional mood because of his troubles at school, and she decided it was best to calm down and agree that Henry should make lunch. He made an elaborate meal of Chinese dumplings and fish, though by now neither Jan nor Alex wanted anything to eat. As he prepared the food, Henry explained that he had become an almost total ascetic: he no longer ate meat, drank alcohol, or smoked cigarettes or cannabis. He said he felt the better for this self-denial because "I'm not polluting my body anymore."

The original plan had been for Alex to spend the night in Henry's room, while Jan would stay with friends about twenty miles away. She was nervous about going ahead with this because Henry was acting so strangely, but she finally agreed to it. Surprisingly, it went well; Henry and Alex got on fine together. The next day she came back, and all three of them went out to lunch at Henry's favourite café. Going there, Henry insisted on walking on the other side of the street from Jan and Alex. In the café, Henry could scarcely stop talking, mostly about eco-lifestyles.

"Everybody should live only in the daylight, get up at dawn, and go to bed at dusk. We should not get our orders from clocks."

"Do you really think clocks tell us what to do, Henry?" asked Alex, who always had a highly rational mind.

"Yes."

Alex pointed to Jan's wristwatch. "But this is an inanimate object. It cannot give orders."

Henry looked at them mulishly, drawing his eyebrows together, as if his mother and brother were in a conspiracy not to understand him. The visit ended amicably enough, but the following day Jan told her therapist about how Henry had behaved. The therapist was alarmed and said that to her it sounded like he was heading for a psychotic breakdown: "He needs to see a psychiatrist as soon as possible and be put on medication." But even after the weekend, Jan could not quite take in what was happening. No more did I. She had told me on the satellite phone to Afghanistan that Henry was walking around barefoot in the middle of the English winter. I replied, "But that's crazy." I meant that his behaviour was weird and irrational, not that I thought he was showing the symptoms of a general mental breakdown.

Henry's final decline was very swift. When Jan had let Alex stay overnight with Henry in his room, she had insisted that he reassemble his mobile phone so she could make contact with him. But as soon as she and Alex had gone back to Canterbury on Sunday afternoon, Henry dismantled it again as part of his general suspicion of all things mechanical and electronic. Over the next few days Jan called him again and again on the landline at the Phoenix hall, but failed to reach him or anybody else. Close to panic, she called Brighton University to find out whether they knew where he was. As if the strain of coping with her son's disappearance were not great enough, Jan found herself the victim of an infuriating official secretiveness masked by a pretended concern for the rights of the ordinary citizen. Asked about Henry, officials at Brighton University said they could not tell Jan anything because of the Data Protection Act. This was a law brought in in 1998 to protect an individual's privacy by banning an official body from disclosing information without his or her consent. The law was notoriously misused by many branches of government – such as police, hospitals, and universities – to refuse to dispense any information about anybody at any time.

In Henry's case, Brighton University was refusing to say what had happened to him until they had his permission to do so. In the interim, Jan went through an agonising time, since she knew the officials would be citing the act only if something were very wrong with Henry, but she did not know what it was. Only on Friday morning, Henry having given his permission, did the university call Jan to say that he was in the Priory Hospital in Hove, a twin town to Brighton, and had been there since Thursday evening. Aghast at hearing that her son had almost died and was being held in a mental hospital, she called the Priory and was able to speak to Henry. He sounded remote and subdued. Asked if he wanted anything, he would say only that he would like some nuts, but, he added, there must be no raisins with them. An hour later, I called from Kabul, and Jan told me what had happened.

It was not possible for Jan to go immediately to Brighton, about 120 miles or a two-hour drive from Canterbury. She had to cancel a lecture she was due to give on women's poetry at Birkbeck College in London, to the voluble dismay of the organiser. There was also Alex to be considered. Jan decided to go to the Priory the next morning, Saturday, after Alex had gone to school at King's. She brought a basket full of things for Henry, including the nuts – pistachios and hazelnuts – that he had asked for. She also brought him some wild-flowers she had picked in a wood near Canterbury where they flowered early. There were primroses, purple violets, and bright yellow celandines, all wrapped in damp moss to keep them fresh. Jan had lunch with some friends in Brighton to fortify herself for her visit to the Priory, a private group of hospitals specialising in mental health care, where visiting hours started at two P.M. The friends suggested that Henry would need toiletries, such as a toothbrush, toothpaste, a facecloth, shower gel, and deodorant. He had grown a beard, so there was no need for a razor. Jan also brought a book, because like me, she read books all the time and felt that being shut up with nothing to read would be a nightmare for Henry, worse even than not having a toothbrush. In the past, he had never read as much as Jan, Alex, or me, but he liked to read occasionally, and when he did so, it was never trash. For instance, if he read a detective story, it would be Raymond Chandler, not Agatha Christie, and this may explain why he had always written fluently. Jan was not sure if he would like a novel, but he had liked poetry in the past, so she found for him an anthology called *101 Happy Poems* by Wendy Cope.

Henry was pleased to see Jan but did not want to speak much. His reception of the presents Jan brought threw into relief his likes and dislikes in the wake of his breakdown. He hungrily ate the nuts he had asked for but was completely uninterested in the spring flowers and the toiletries. His illness would come to be associated with mess, not just untidiness but an attraction to detritus, to smelly alleyways and heaps of rubbish. Jan's touching gift of spring flowers was added to a small heap of refuse, consisting mostly of old orange peel and crisps packets, which Henry had already placed on the floor of his neat room. He did not want anybody to touch the pile, to which he added Jan's carefully gathered flowers, so they soon withered. The book interested him more, and he looked pleased to have been given it, though he did not actually read any poems. Henry said very little to Jan during that first visit, which went on for about three hours. But he did have one unexpected request which surprised her. It was for her to sing to him a protest hymn by James Russell Lowell, the nineteenth-century New England poet, critic, and anti-slavery advocate, called "Once to Every Man and Nation." Henry had heard it many times in the past because, although Jan was not religious herself, her father was an Anglican clergyman, and hymn singing was very much part of her background. Thanks to her excellent memory, she recalled the words of these hymns, and when Henry and Alex were too young for storybooks, she would sing the hymns as lullabies. On one long, boring drive back from Ireland a year earlier, Henry had asked Jan to sing the hymn again. Now in the hospital, he asked her to sing the hymn "that you sang when we were coming back from Ireland." Jan sang it to him, and he asked her to sing it again and again until she had done so five times. Two of its verses go:

> *Once to every man and nation,*
> *Comes the moment to decide*
> *In the strife of truth with falsehood*
> *For the good or evil side.*
> *Some great cause, God's new Messiah,*
> *Offering each the bloom or blight.*
> *And the choice goes by for ever*
> *'Twixt that darkness and that light.*

> *Then to side with truth is noble*
> *While we share her wretched crust,*
> *Ere her cause bring fame and profit.*
> *And 'tis prosperous to be just.*
> *Then it is the brave man chooses,*
> *While the coward stands aside,*
> *Till the multitude make virtue*
> *Of the faith they had denied.*

Why did Henry, who never showed any sign of being religious, find the hymn so appealing at this dire moment in his life? Probably because it reminded him of a happy childhood. But perhaps he wanted to hear it so many times because it speaks of a "new Messiah," and he felt he had been given a special message, though he did not really know what this was. Above all, Lowell's fine hymn has as its theme the choice of good over evil and of standing up against the forces of darkness. Its words chime in with Henry's feeling that the voices he heard and the visions he had seen – but was only beginning to speak about to other people – were not delusions or hallucinations but real and revelatory. Far from going mad or being mentally ill, he was entering a brave, new, and magical world.

CHAPTER TWO

Patrick

I stayed overnight in Canterbury and had breakfast with Jan before taking a taxi to Brighton to see Henry. I told her that I planned to stay down there until we knew what was going to happen to him. Jan's account of the disastrous weekend when she and Alex went to see him had left me prepared to find him completely changed, even crazed. At the same time, I could not bring myself to believe that Henry's distinct and lively personality had been completely submerged by a mental disorder. I stopped briefly in Brighton to check in to a hotel called the Old Ship, overlooking the seafront. I chose it because it was the first hotel I saw, and I wanted to get rid of my suitcase before going to see Henry.

The hospital was smaller than I had expected, a private clinic rather than a large-scale facility, housed in a gloomy Victorian mansion in Hove. I was desperate to see Henry; irrationally, I felt that if I did so, all would come right in the end. The Priory staff was friendly and helpful but had the slightly forced cheeriness I had often noticed in people looking after the sick. There was nothing to show that I was in a mental hospital other than frequent locked doors that opened with a code. A nurse took me to the third floor and showed me into Henry's attic room. He was standing in the middle of the room, looking lonely and baffled, but his face lit up when he saw me, and we embraced. I asked him how he was and what had happened to him, and he said that he had felt the urge to walk barefoot back to his old home in Canterbury and had been picked up by fishermen when he got out of the water at Newhaven.

"The doctors put you in here because they are worried that you might have been trying to kill yourself," I said as casually as I could, though I very much wanted to find out if it was true. I had been told moments earlier by the nurses that one of them came to see Henry every twenty minutes "to see that he is all right." I assumed it was a relaxed suicide watch, since presumably, a nurse would have been watching Henry the whole time if they thought there was a real danger of him killing himself.

"No, I wasn't trying to commit suicide," said Henry firmly and with some exasperation, as if he had already been asked the question too many times. Everything he said about his recent experiences turned out to be accurate insofar as it went, but I later realised that it left many things out. When I asked him gently why he thought he was in the Priory, he said without any sign of resentment that he felt the police and the doctors had misunderstood and overreacted to his eccentric lifestyle.

I did not want to press Henry too hard about what had happened; I could see that he was in a fragile mental condition. For several hours I sat on the narrow single bed in his room while he lay on the floor. He seemed comforted by my presence. Sometimes he beat out a rhythm on the bottom of an upturned wastepaper bin and chanted snatches of rap, which seemed to be a new interest, but mostly, he was listless and apathetic. He replied when I asked him something but otherwise said very little. During this first meeting, I was so overjoyed to see him alive that I did not try to work out how ill he was other than asking him if he had wanted to kill himself.

After promising to come back the following day, I had a brief meeting with Dr Duncan Angus, the consultant psychiatrist. He spoke cautiously about Henry's condition, saying he might be in the initial phase of schizophrenia, but he had not made a final diagnosis and would not do so for ten days. During that time, Henry would be under observation. The word "schizophrenia" did not mean very much to me, since I knew almost nothing about the illness except that it did not mean having a split personality. I had spent many months in general hospitals in Cork and London after I got polio forty-five years earlier, but I had never been inside a mental hospital in my life. I asked what the prognosis was for Henry if it was confirmed that he had schizophrenia. Dr Angus said that in such a case, the usual medical nostrum was that "a third of people diagnosed with schizophrenia recover completely, one third have further attacks but show improvement, and one third do not get better." I told him that I was staying on in Brighton and asked if I could take Henry out. Rather to my surprise, he said that this would be all right, so long as Henry always stayed with me.

I visited Henry every day for the rest of that week. Sometimes we would sit in his room in the Priory or have lunch in the cafeteria on the ground floor. Mostly, we would go out, taking long walks along the seafront and eating in one of Brighton's many restaurants. During these days I began to see changes in Henry that had not struck me the first day. He was averse to cleanliness or orderliness of any kind, something that Jan had noticed at the art college. In the Priory, he evidently disliked wearing shoes, socks, or underpants and even had to be prompted to flush the lavatory after he used it. He was wary of anything mechanical or electronic, such as watches and mobile phones, and was suspicious that the smoke alarm in one corner of his room was monitoring him. As we talked for hour after hour, at first inside the Priory and later on during our walks, I became familiar with Henry's new mental landscape. The transformation was not complete, and many things about him were the same as ever, but every so often there were fleeting references to visions and voices. Henry was probably being circumspect because he did not think I would believe him, and he was level-headed enough to see that the more he spoke about them, the more likely it was that the doctors would keep him locked up. Instead of describing his visions and voices in detail, he spoke vaguely of religious and mystical forces, often using the imagery of *The Lord of the Rings* – with its goblins and demons plotting against mankind in their dark holes beneath the surface of the earth – to express paranoid fears of prosaic objects. Often he would ask me if I thought there might be secret tunnels under Brighton.

When I was not with Henry, I was online in my room in the Old Ship, trying to learn as much as I could about schizophrenia. Jan stayed in Canterbury because she had to work, look after Alex, and recover from having dealt alone with the mounting crisis over Henry while I was still in Afghanistan. I read scientific papers and summaries, many from the National Institute of Mental Health in the US, with increasing dismay. I discovered that an American doctor had described schizophrenia as being to mental illness what cancer is to physical ailments. The average age for the onset of schizophrenia is eighteen for men and twenty-five for women. Henry had had his twentieth birthday on January 4, 2002, which corresponded with the first time Jan had noticed he was behaving oddly. There were said to be 250,000 diagnosed cases of schizophrenia in Britain, though the true figure may be closer to half a million, if the undiagnosed are included. In the world, some 51 million people are estimated to have the illness, of which 2.2 million are in the US. I read that symptoms do not include violence, but the suicide rate is very high, and people with the condition attempt suicide fifty times more frequently than the general population. I began to understand why nurses kept dodging in and out of Henry's room to make sure he was not harming himself.

All this made gloomy reading, but I felt a slight sense of comfort as I saw all the solid-looking statistics: the information might help Jan and me find the best way to help him. I did not grasp that schizophrenia is a much vaguer concept than I imagined. Though symptoms could be alleviated or controlled by drugs developed since the 1950s, treatment seemed to be at about the level of treatment of physical sickness a century earlier. Medications might work, but it is not clear precisely why, or why they are effective for one person but not for another. The causes of schizophrenia have been the subject of prolonged, rancorous, and inconclusive debate among scientists. I read that people generally develop the disorder because they are genetically predisposed to do so and doctors invariably asked the victims if anybody else in their families had been mentally ill. Dr Angus had asked me this when I saw him. But genes are not solely responsible for the disorder. Tests show that if one of a set of wholly identical twins develops schizophrenia, the other twin has a 50 percent chance of becoming a schizophrenic as well. But the second twin has a 50 per cent chance of *not* developing the illness. This must mean that there are other forces at work, such as events in the life of a person at risk, that determine if he or she will develop schizophrenia. Its onset might be brought on by some stressful personal disaster, like the loss of a job, academic failure, the breakdown of a love affair, or the death of a relative. Or it might, as many studies appeared to prove, be the result of mind-altering street drugs such as cannabis or skunk, a more powerful form of cannabis.

All this was interesting but did not do Henry much good in the short term. Leaving aside any mental disorder, being locked inside a mental hospital was enough to depress anybody. I did what I could to raise his morale. We spent a lot of time in the Lanes, the narrow streets filled with self-consciously bohemian shops and restaurants. Henry ran into an astonishing number of friends whom he had met during his first year at art college. I was pleased by this, since he had complained that none of his friends came to see him at the Priory. But when he did see them – and they all seemed delighted at a chance meeting – he would end the conversation after a few minutes of friendly talk, politely refuse to join them for a drink, and say we had to go. I thought he was ashamed to say he was in a mental hospital, which was understandable, but he also seemed to be withdrawing into himself, a more ominous sign which I had read was a well-known symptom of schizophrenia. Even when we were together, Henry often walked ten yards in front of me, and I had to stumble after him to keep up. I felt a constant underlying anxiety because, although I thought it unlikely he would run away, I was not absolutely sure. Sometimes I would lose sight of him and would endure a surge of panic until he reappeared.

I told him I had lived in Brighton for a few months when I was about five and had not enjoyed it because I was used to living in the middle of the lush Irish countryside, building tree houses and damming small streams with rocks and mud. I much preferred the long sandy Irish beaches with interesting cliffs to climb, and rock pools with shrimps hiding in the seaweed to investigate, compared to Brighton, with its heaped-up banks of pebbles which were so hard on the toes. One thing I had enjoyed as a child in 1955 was walking along the pier with my nanny, Kitty Lee, whose funeral Henry had gone to in December. When Kitty and I reached the far end of the pier, we would visit a glass case containing a toy bear who cheerily drank a glass of beer when a penny was put in the slot. Henry and I tried to find the place where the hard-drinking bear had once stood, but Brighton pier, with its ornate white pleasure palace on top, was collapsing into the sea, and there were large notices warning of danger and forbidding anybody to set foot on it.

Jan and I anxiously awaited the crucial meeting with Dr Angus, when he would present his diagnosis and ask Henry voluntarily to take an anti-psychotic drug. Jan took two days off work and drove down to Brighton so we could prepare for it. The diagnosis was not our main worry because we were almost certain Dr Angus was going to say that Henry was in the prodromal, or incipient, phase of schizophrenia. There is no physical or laboratory test for the disorder, such as blood tests or imaging of the brain, so the diagnosis is based on identifying a number of different symptoms. In Henry's case, all too many were obviously present. Talking to him every day, I felt as if part of his brain was in overdrive and part in underdrive. The overdrive signs, which the psychiatrists call "positive" symptoms, were the most striking and included voices that came from trees and bushes; hallucinations which Henry believed were visions; and delusions, frequently paranoid, such as the suspicion that Brighton sits on a network of tunnels concealing dark forces. His thinking was sometimes disordered, and he would change topics at random. The underdrive, which psychiatrists describe as "negative" symptoms, was less obvious but included apathy, when he would stare into the middle distance; inability to react to other people even when they were glad to see him; and distaste for washing, keeping clean, or being fully dressed. It was as if he saw the world through a strange distorting mirror, though the degree of distortion changed by the day and by the hour.

Jan and I were worried about the meeting with Dr Angus less because of his diagnosis than Henry's reaction to it. We knew that his best chance of escaping from schizophrenia depended on early diagnosis and appropriate medication. But since Henry did not accept that there was anything wrong with him, it was highly doubtful that he would take whatever anti-psychotic drug the doctor prescribed. He had made clear to us that he considered his presence in the Priory unnecessary. A few days before the meeting, we had talked to Dr Angus about persuading Henry that it was in his best interest to take the medication, which we learned would be olanzapine. We were told that if Henry agreed to take the olanzapine, he would be classed an "informal" patient, meaning one who accepts being in the hospital and whatever treatment he receives. He would largely be a free agent and could even leave the hospital when he wanted. But if he refused to take the olanzapine, he would be "sectioned" – that is, detained under Section 3 of the Mental Health Act as somebody who is a danger to himself, the evidence being his climbing of the viaduct in Brighton and swimming the estuary in Newhaven.

Jan and I picked up Henry from the Priory the day before the meeting with Dr Angus. We went for a long walk with him along the seafront. It was a particularly chilly day, with low clouds and spitting rain. We stopped in a depressing little memorial garden of leafless rosebushes with a monument for the dead of the two world wars and sat there in the drizzle. I said to Henry, "I know you've had a terrible time in the last few weeks, and you find the Priory depressing, but we think the olanzapine will make you feel better, and it is your best chance of coming home."

"I won't take it because there is nothing wrong with me," Henry replied quietly but adamantly. We tried all our well-rehearsed arguments, appealing to him to take the drug because it was beneficial, and at the end of the day, he would have to take it anyway. Henry was polite but firm: he was not going to take the anti-psychotic.

I said, "The reason I got polio was that there was no vaccine available in Ireland at the time, but if there had been and I had taken it, I would have been all right. The olanzapine is your equivalent of the polio vaccine."

"But you were really ill, and I am not," said Henry. I shied away from pursuing the comparison between my polio and his schizophrenia. It was not an entirely fair argument, since the polio vaccine really did stop people from getting the disease, while the olanzapine, however much good it might do Henry, was not a cure-all for his illness.

The argument seemed to go on for hours. At one moment Henry walked away from us and stood by a low concrete wall, looking out at the sea. Jan and I remained sitting on a wooden bench by the war memorial. She said to me, "He won't do it because he feels he is defending his whole identity and integrity, and taking the drugs means that everything he thinks is wrong." I remembered that to Henry, his voices and visions were quite real, and what he heard and saw was often beautiful and revelatory. We thought it was pointless to go on pressing him to take medication, the purpose of which was to banish these dreams, when he was so determined not to do so.

The next day, the meeting took place in Henry's attic room, which was slightly too small for the four of us. As we expected, the doctor said Henry was in the incipient stage of schizophrenia, citing various symptoms. He said that Henry should take olanzapine, and if he did so and showed signs of responding to the drug, then he would be free to leave the Priory. Henry calmly replied that he would not take the medication because there was nothing wrong with him. We repeated all the arguments of the previous day, and he rejected them. I thought we were getting nowhere. Finally, Jan began to weep, saying, "I can't take this anymore. I can't face the fact, Henry, that you may never get well."

There was a very long pause while nobody said anything. Jan looked embarrassed about breaking down. Then Henry, more moved by his mother's distress than all our urgings, said, "Well, all right, then, I will take the olanzapine."

As we left the Priory, Jan said to me she was sorry for crying, and I replied, "If there ever was a good time to break down, that was it."

Henry started to take his medication, but it would be several weeks before we would know if it was having any effect. There was nothing much I could do to help except keep him company, though this was beginning to wear me down. I found Brighton's pretensions to off-season gaiety increasingly hard to take, though, to be fair, no place on earth would have felt sympathetic under the circumstances, and the English Channel is not an enticing place in February. When Henry and I first started walking around Brighton, there were some bright chill days when the sea was a sparkling blue, but the weather soon turned to dark clouds and rain, and the colour of the sea was a depressing mud-grey.

I was one of a very few guests at the Old Ship, a friendly enough establishment, of which my main memory is that it was filled with hundreds of unread copies of *The Daily Telegraph*, delivered free to the almost empty hotel as if it were the height of the season and packed with prospective readers. The sight of the neatly folded white newspapers on every flat surface reminded me of a famous scene in Alfred Hitchcock's film *The Birds* when a visitor looks out the door of a house to see silent and immobile birds perched menacingly on every roof, fence, and telephone wire. I told Henry about this, and we laughed at the idea of unread newspapers plotting to take over my hotel. In general, I found it hard to be unrelentingly cheerful and optimistic because there were so few signs of Henry getting better.

I soon got a sense of what Henry found attractive and what he did not like. He preferred small things to large. I took him to see the Royal Pavilion, the exotic palace built for the Prince Regent with its Indian-style Mogul domes and minarets outside and golden Chinese dragons and imitation palm trees inside. Henry dutifully walked round it, but he much preferred talking to a beggar in the garden outside and studying the twisted shape of pieces of driftwood thrown up by the sea on the beach. There were good days and bad. I was becoming physically and mentally exhausted. Even before Henry had his breakdown, I was tired from covering the Afghan war. But whenever I saw Henry interested in and able to accomplish small practical tasks, this tiredness would evaporate. Once I felt encouraged when I saw Henry find a lost mobile phone that a man was desperately searching for in the shingle on the beach. This was a practical, rational thing to do. But my morale would slump when I saw Henry attracted by dark alleys and heaps of rubbish, which he would often want to use as a lavatory. Once I bought him a large green mango as we walked back to the Priory and watched with despair as he tore at it with his teeth, juice and pieces of fruit smearing his unshaved face as he gobbled it down like a hungry animal.

"Do you think I am mad?" Henry would occasionally ask me sadly and with real anxiety as we strolled about. I never quite knew how to answer. So much turned on Henry recognising that he was ill and taking medication, which might not cure his psychosis but might at least control it. Though he might deny there was anything wrong with him, he sensed he was not well. But as Jan had recognised when we were persuading him to take his olanzapine, he resisted doing anything that would deny the magical reality of his

visions and voices. It was significant that he would not take medication if it meant labelling his experiences as fantasies requiring treatment, but he would do so to stop his mother crying. His affection for
his family never wavered.

I found it difficult to answer Henry's question about whether or
not he was mad partly because I did not want to upset him. I would
nervously fudge the answer, saying something like: "You are not
exactly mad, but you are not in your right mind part of the time." I
was also coming to see that the distinction between sane and insane
was much woollier and more ambivalent than I had previously
realised. "Madness" or "insanity" is not a concrete description of
an identifiable ailment but the sum total of a kaleidoscope of symptoms. In trying to understand what was wrong with Henry, I was
surprised and rather appalled by my own ignorance of mental illness. I had read Sigmund Freud when I was a student at Oxford,
but in this case, he was of singularly little help, since he dealt primarily with neurosis rather than psychosis. His picture of how the
mind worked seemed to bear little relation to my own experiences
with Henry. The ignorance of many of my generation about mental health was rooted in part in the traditional fear of madness and
a superficial knowledge of psychoanalysis. Of course, there were
those who knew a great deal about mental illness, because they had
relatives who suffered from the disorder, but they seldom talked
about it.

Early in March, just before my fifty-second birthday, Dr Angus
told me that Henry was responding to the medication. It seemed he
was not part of the one third of schizophrenic patients who never
recover from the first onset of the illness. I phoned Jan to pass on the
glad news, but, pleased though we were, we were coming to understand that schizophrenia was a calamity from which there would be
no swift escape. We could see now, as we had not a few short weeks

earlier when Henry first began behaving strangely, that mental illness was a mysterious, ill-defined disorder, wholly different from physical ills like tuberculosis or cholera, which could be cured with the right medicine. The olanzapine we had taken such trouble to persuade Henry to take was not going to cure him. Jan and I began to see that it would be easy to burn oneself out emotionally, physically, and financially in trying to bring comfort to Henry in the short term, while in fact we were facing a lifetime's struggle.

CHAPTER THREE
Henry

The first time I heard the word "schizophrenic" was in an arts class at King's School in Canterbury and somebody had done a series of good drawings. The teacher said they "looked like the paintings of a schizophrenic." I had an idea at the time that schizophrenia meant a split personality. I heard the word again after I swam the estuary at Newhaven, and I heard it used in the hospital. Some fishermen took me there, saying I had hypothermia. The doctor told me it was common for people of my age to have mental illness. I didn't think of it as an illness but as an awakening, a spiritual awakening. I thought there was another side to the world I hadn't seen before.

I had started out that morning from my art college, a tall building opposite the market near the London Road in Brighton, walking barefoot along the edge of the sea. I went east towards my home in Canterbury. I felt brambles, trees, and wild animals all urging me on. It was as if they were looking at me and I could feel what they thought. Once I stopped and went to a little spring and washed myself. I walked along the seashore beside a high seawall holding back the cliffs. The wall

seemed a hundred feet high. I believed there were prisoners behind
it, and I sang to them.

I walked ten miles, sometimes going by the seashore and sometimes
across fields. Once I was tempted to steal a motorcycle I saw beside the
road, but a voice told me not to. As I entered Newhaven, I saw the letter D painted on the road, and I thought this meant D for "daemon," so
I ran down an alleyway. I knocked on an orange-coloured door. It was
opened by an old lady, and I asked her the way out.

When I was in Newhaven, I hid under a heap of ladders. I felt
that people were following me. I went to the estuary and hid by a low
wall. I didn't want to go into the water at first, but finally, I did get
in and heard somebody shout: "You stupid bastard!" I thought I was
going to die. I saw brambles everywhere. It was about twenty yards
across, and after I got out on the other side, it was freezing. I was
underneath a jetty, and there were steel girders. It was so cold that
I went back in the water, and I was there when a fisherman held out
his hand. The next thing I remember, I was in an ambulance with no
windows, being taken to the hospital in Brighton. I felt it was underground. I remember an alcoholic being in the bed next to me, eating
a lot of ham sandwiches. He gave me a couple of them. I was there
for a day, and at first it was okay, but then they checked up on me and
thought I might want to commit suicide. One of the doctors said,
"I have some good news for you." I thought he meant I was going
home. He said, "No, you are going to the Priory." I suppose he must
have meant that the Priory was better than a general mental hospital.

When I arrived in Hove, I thought it was a bit bland but pleasantly
multicultural, with lots of black doctors. One of them asked if I felt I
was on television, with everybody watching me. I knew that what he
meant was "Do you feel intense paranoia?" In fact, I had been feeling just that, but as soon as I heard him say so, I realised I was not on
television. Later, I saw the chief psychiatrist, who seemed to me like

an alien being. "Have you ever seen a psychiatrist before?" he asked. "I might have," I replied. "I suspect you haven't, because you would remember it," he said. I asked his name. He said, "Dr Duncan Angus." I asked, "Can I call you Duncan?" "No," he said firmly. He asked if he could contact my parents and tell them what had happened to me, and I said that he could.

That night I had a confused dream about rugby which left me feeling I was controlled by the system. Afterwards I went down to the breakfast room on the ground floor, where I ate oatmeal with bananas – the same breakfast I was to have every morning I was in the Priory. I went back upstairs to the smoking room, the main room for socialising in the house. There was a man there who told me, "If you want to get out of here, the best thing you can do is to attend the groups." I found these groups of patients discussing their problems deeply boring, but he was probably right.

My mother came to see me and hugged me. My father called from Afghanistan and said, "The main thing is not to worry." I remember going to the top floor of the building, where I could open one of the windows through which I might have escaped, but I didn't quite have the gall to run away. When I was in my room, a nurse kept poking her head around the door, which seemed a bit strange. I found a metal wastepaper basket in the corner of my room and used it as a drum. I made up a song to go along with the drumbeats which went: "Through and through and on to Peru / Through every taboo and on to Peru." I had been in Peru for my cousin's wedding the year before.

Now that I find myself in a mental hospital, I look back on my first days in Brighton as the best days of my life. I liked the beach, the architecture, the college, the sunsets. When I went there the previous

summer to apply to Brighton Art College, all I knew about the city
was that it was supposed to be an exciting, bustling place. The first
time I saw it, it was night-time. I walked the empty streets by myself
and could see the clubs from the outside, but I did not go into any. I
was scared they'd throw me out because I looked young for my age,
which was nineteen at the time. I stopped to give money to a tramp
with a bottle of cider beside him who was sitting on the pavement.
I told him that I was thinking of coming to Brighton, and he said
I'd enjoy it, that there were plenty of parties going on, and lots of
women.

I showed the people at the art college my dilapidated portfolio,
mostly faces I had done with acrylic paints, and they said they would
give me a place. They asked what I would do when I left college,
and I said I was going to open a café. I had spent the previous year at
Wimbledon College of Art in south London, and after that I worked
for two months at an Indian restaurant called Bombay Bicycle in
south London, taking orders for food from five to eleven at night.
Back then I was free, free to walk where I pleased, yet I wasn't particularly happy. I wasn't confident about myself, around women, or
even when I was in a large group of people.

I had heard that Brighton was a gay capital, but it seemed to me
to be full of beautiful women. My student flat had five women and
three boys, including me. I made many friends and got on well with
my housemates, though later, I was sad that none of them rang me up
when I was in the hospital. After the tiny room in Wimbledon when
I did my foundation year, my new room felt huge. I remember walking the Brighton streets at night. I discovered basketball hoops, and
the next day I went and bought a basketball. One day I played a few
games, and when I got back to college, I saw a beautiful girl called
Elisa, one of my flatmates whom I had talked to before but did not
really know. We decided to go for a walk. She said she had a cold, so

we went to the nearest chemist. Then we walked down towards the seafront. It was a beautiful blue day. We went to a pub, and after that we smoked half a joint. She said she wanted to laugh more than she'd ever laughed before. We walked towards the setting sun. And I sang, I sang to her, I sang more than I'd ever sung before. I used to make up little ditties when I went for walks on the cliff tops in Ireland. I'd never sung them to anybody before. I asked her to kiss me, but she said no. We walked and walked and walked. She walked across the cobblestones where there was a small patch of sand, and she took off her shoes and started dancing. I had never seen anything so beautiful before. I lay down on the cobbled stones, and after a while I could hear feet walking towards me. I got up and saw her, and we walked back along the seafront without saying anything. Eventually, we could see lights, but she pointed out that they were from the new pier, shining through the wreck of the old abandoned one. I still had my basketball with me. It felt so cumbersome, but I didn't throw it away. I asked if she knew anything about Buddhism because she had orange trousers on. When we got back, we both went to our rooms separately.

I liked the graffiti on the walls in Brighton. I was always good at art, and I was highly influenced by Jean-Michel Basquiat. His style was mainly of symbols and signs, and in his paintings I caught a whiff of magic. I found an all-night café that had just opened. It was designed to catch people drifting in after a night's heavy clubbing. I said I had some pictures and asked if they would like to put them on the walls. They said they would, and I went back to get my paintings. I felt I was following in the footsteps of Basquiat, who had famously gained notoriety by selling postcards of his work to Andy Warhol, thus showing he was not just a graffiti artist. Basquiat later became contemptuous of graffiti art, but I liked it because it was rough and raw.

I always said I wanted to be a political cartoonist, but I think this was mostly to please my dad. As a kid I used to look at graffiti from trains as the walls on which it was painted darted past, and I dreamed of painting the walls myself. Once a friend and I went to a village on the outskirts of Brighton where graffiti artists were painting pictures on the inside of a big warehouse. There was a lot of broken glass and rusting metal on the floor. The warehouse was shrouded in mist, and we couldn't see the people doing the graffiti until we had walked about halfway towards them. I borrowed one of their cans and did a piece on an abandoned wall. The only graffiti I have done since has been on the walls of smoking rooms in hospitals, but they have all been painted over, and it would take an archaeological investigation to find them.

At Brighton during that first term, my painting had become circular, and I was trying to break away from that. A few weeks later, I was in Ireland, where I picked up a copy of a book on Jackson Pollock. It said he was possessed by daemons, and when an artist starts drawing circles, it is the first sign of madness. I firmly shut the book because I believed that some ghost in the cottage I was reading it in was trying to tell me I was mad. I saw myself as a direct descendant of artists from Basquiat to Picasso. Was it just a dream I had a long time ago, or was I as good as I thought? For a kid growing up, the world is a complicated place.

I went to Ireland for three days at the beginning of December because Kitty Lee, my father's nanny whom I had known all my life, had just died. The porter at the student block of flats where I was living woke me up to tell me about it. The day after Kitty died, I made a small offering under a tree with, among other things, a little K – a magnetic letter like you stick on the fridge. I was not very sad because her death had been easy, and I can hear her voice still in my head. I do not mind this because I know she would never hurt me.

I walked in her funeral down the main street in Youghal, the town in County Cork where she lived. I left some orange flowers in a pot on her grave. Beside it there was lichen growing on the cement, and John King, a friend from Ardmore, the village where we had a house, said to me that "lichen only grows where the air is clean."

I went back to Ireland for Christmas, and it was when I returned to Brighton that my life changed. I did not see many people, was often by myself, gave up smoking cannabis and cigarettes, became a vegan, and took to walking around barefoot. I had been drinking a lot during my first term, mostly beer. Looking back, I spent most of my time at college in a stoned, drunken haze. I took a lot of marijuana between the ages of fourteen and nineteen. I was quite shy and inhibited, and I had always seen myself as a bit of a rich kid. I went to a public school and had lived abroad in Russia from the age of three to five, then in America when I was a bit older. Other than that, I had lived all my life in Canterbury, where I had both public school friends and local friends. It was through drugs that I met these friends, many of whom went to Brighton, unlike my friends from King's School. My teenage years would have been different without marijuana. Did I take more of it than others? Not really. Why did we smoke so much? Maybe it was because the music scene, which I wanted to be part of, was drug-oriented. My generation smoked more dope than the one before. I was taking a lot of hash, maybe an eighth of an ounce, which cost ten pounds. It would have been better if I hadn't, but about half the people I knew in Canterbury were smoking dope. I took skunk, but not very often. It tastes different and is not very nice.

The worst thing about smoking weed when you are a kid is that you never really grow up. Your life turns into a sort of haze. I think I would have grown up a lot quicker without the weed. On the flip side, as I said, you meet a lot of people, but when you do meet them, you don't really talk to them. I was naturally quite shy, and getting stoned made things worse. I'd go to somebody's house and start off quite talkative, and then, after the first joint, you'd be lucky to hear another word out of me. Most of my family and friends believe that my being sectioned was because of drugs.

In Ireland I had thought about walking to Tibet barefoot, and when I got back to Brighton, I did not wear shoes much because I wanted to harden the soles of my feet, like Mowgli in *The Jungle Book*. In fact they didn't grow hard, but they did become calloused and numb. It is amazing the number of people who stare at you when you are not wearing shoes. If I were to dye my hair green, I probably would not get the same attention. Admittedly, it was the middle of winter when I started walking to college barefoot, which might explain why people were so surprised. I can't quite remember why I became a vegan, since I like eating meat, particularly duck. I thought I should pretend to be deaf and blind so my senses would get better.

It was about this time I had my first vision. I had borrowed a book on meditation and was sitting on the beach in Brighton in the lotus position, trying to meditate. It was only for a few seconds, but I saw two birds fly across each other, and where they crossed, I saw a golden Buddha in the sky. I was wearing shoes for once, but I took them off. I started to climb the earth embankment by the sea because I thought the Hanging Gardens of Babylon were on the other side. Later, I felt I wanted to stare death in the face and started to climb on top of a high wall overlooking the railway track. People shouted at me to get down, and when I did so, one of them bought me an orange juice. But they also called the police, who asked if I was trying to kill myself. I said I just wanted to get a better view of Brighton. They also asked me, "Have you seen things?" I did not tell them about the golden Buddha. The police were good to me, though I thought it was a bit much to be arrested mainly for having bare feet.

My brother, Alex, was coming down to Brighton to see me. I wanted to make a drum for him. I left college in search of clay for it. I decided I would not consult a map or ask anyone the way but would try to find clay using just my senses. I was wearing my best clothes: the trousers of a suit my grandfather had given me and a black and blue jumper with a dash of red and white around the arms. It was a cold but clear day, the sky a light blue, and as I walked, I tried not to think of anything, as if I were meditating, and to control the words that came into my head. People stared at me as I walked, and one person jeered at me as a "crackhead." They had no idea that I had given up even coffee. I came to a shop called Evolution, which had a sign in the shape of two interlacing spirals. I thought this would be a place where I could pick up some clay. I went round the back and there was a woman there. I asked her if she would do clay classes. She said they were on Thursday, and I replied that this was too late because my brother was coming on Sunday. I said I had a record player that I could use as a potter's wheel. She looked at me, stupefied, and got out a big bag of clay and dumped it on the table. I picked it up and left. As I walked back, I picked up pieces of wood for the drum and tried holding my breath for as long as I could. I saw white birds like seagulls flying inland and black crows flying towards the sea. I followed the white birds.

I found myself walking on a road parallel to the train tracks. I felt I was going on a mission. You know fire hydrants are yellow and have an H on them. I thought the H stood for Henry. I climbed a barbed-wire fence and sat under a big tree. I put down all the stuff I had amassed: bits of metal, bits of wood, and a big bag of clay. I felt the tree telling me to take off my shoes. I was scared, as I had been arrested previously for not wearing shoes. I climbed over another barbed-wire fence and found myself in the undergrowth beside the railway track. A train went past and I was in full view. I found my

way under the root of a tree and could feel it talking to me in my
head. A dog barked, and I held my breath for as long as I could until
I soiled myself. I saw flashlights and people looking for me beside
the railway track. The root of the tree moved as it touched me, and
it said I was like Basquiat. It said I could rap, it said I was the best of
rappers.

I was trying to grow plants. I bought a banana tree and planted it
in a basket made out of an upturned lamp shade which I hung outside
the window of my room. Later I transplanted the tree to some good
soil I found outside a club called Concorde 2 on the seafront. I went
and sat in the room of a friend called Keever who had loaned me the
book on meditation. I had walked in barefoot, and he looked disap-
provingly at me. He told me, "You might step on heroin needles and
get HIV." He then said, "People who are poverty-stricken and can't
afford shoes would look at you not wearing shoes and think you were
mocking them. Maybe you are going down alleyways that have dead
ends. You could end up in a mental hospital." The head teacher of
our year in art school told me the same thing, that I might get HIV
by stepping on a heroin needle. *Surely there can't be that many junkies
in Brighton*, I thought.

After talking to the tree, I had thrown away the pieces of wood
and tin I had collected to make the drum for my brother, Alex. I
went searching for them but ended up going completely in the wrong
direction. Everything seemed to want me to leave Brighton, but my
brother was coming down for the weekend, and I felt I couldn't aban-
don him. I started to walk back towards Brighton; it was a very long
way to the block of flats where I lived. Just before I got there, I saw
a red bus go by with the words BLOOD BROTHERS on it, and I thought
this was relevant to me returning to my brother and not going on my
journey out of Brighton. When I got back, my mother was furious
with me for being three hours late. Eventually, she calmed down and

let Alex spend the night with me. I made some Chinese spring rolls with him, and we ate them with my housemates.

Sometimes at the Priory, I felt I was mad and at other times that the magical experiences I had been having were real. I made friends with one of the nurses at the Priory called Claren. She was a big woman; she listened to my experiences more like a friend than a nurse. She told me how she was interested in Buddhism and had discovered a local meditation centre. That night she told me how Australian aborigines put stones in their mouths so they produce saliva and have to drink less under the hot sun. The next day my father and I went to the beach. I thought that Claren's story related to me but in a different way. I recalled that birds have no teeth and swallow stones to digest, so I thought that if I swallowed a stone, I would turn into a bird and be able to fly away from the Priory and all my troubles. I was scared at first that I would choke, but I plucked up my courage and swallowed a black stone and then a grey one. I bought some cockles and swallowed them whole.

One day I decided I'd start smoking again. I had a couple of cigarettes when my dad took me out. The hospital had agreed that we could go for walks together. When I got back, my friend Gregg offered me a spliff. I thought, *What the hell,* and we went into my room to smoke it. Before we sparked it, he said, "Do you know how the system works?" I said no. "Cameras inside televisions," he said. "How do you know?" I asked him. "Have you opened one up?" "Yes," he said. The hospital had taken away the metal waste bin I was using as a drum because they said it was a danger to me. My mother had brought me an Indian bongo drum, and Gregg played it while I sang. Later, he left and went to his room, and I was left looking at the pale yellow wall in my room, which at that moment symbolised for me my sense of being trapped and locked up in a prison cell.

I had been under observation at the Priory. They were trying to see if I was having a psychotic episode. At the end of two weeks, they said they would section me if I refused to take the medication – olanzapine. I was of two minds: first, I didn't agree with it, as I didn't think I was ill but merely spiritually awakened. And second, I didn't agree with taking substances that would affect my mind. On the other hand, I didn't want to be sectioned. Finally, Mum burst into tears, so I had to take it. Even so, I tried to counteract the olanzapine with tobacco by smoking lots of cigarettes because the word began with O and "tobacco" ended with the same letter.

Eventually, the doctors agreed to let me go back to Canterbury for the weekend. I went and bought some fish and two grapefruits to cook. I wanted to go out, but my dad would have none of it. I walked down our street with my dad trailing behind me, saying, "You must come back, you must come back." Eventually, I did. I felt so depressed that night that I wanted to hang myself from a tree. I heard my friend Phil's voice saying, "No, Henry, don't do that." The next day I went to see Phil. I had a small pipe of hash with him. When I got back to Hove, the psychiatrist asked me, "Did you smoke any cannabis?" I thought this was something of a game, so I said no. Later, I decided I would never lie again, whatever the circumstances. The doctor let me go back home at the end of March.

It was at the Priory that I first regularly heard voices from people, rather than from trees and bushes. It was as if I could hear what they were thinking, as if I could hear their thoughts. At the same time, I thought that most of what happened to me at the Priory was persecution. I don't think I was a danger to myself or others. I would have been better off wandering around Brighton. Once you are in the system, it is difficult to escape it. The drugs you are supposed to take – in my case, olanzapine – you are meant to take for years, possibly for life. I did not think I needed them.

Do I have schizophrenia? My mother and father and the dreaded psychiatrist definitely believe I am schizophrenic. They have grounds for their belief, such as my being found naked and talking to trees in woods. Yet I think I just see the world differently from other people, and maybe if psychiatrists understood this, I would not have been in the hospital. When people hear about a psychotic episode, they probably relate the word "psycho" to someone with violent tendencies. I would not describe myself as violent. I have really felt the strain of being in the hospital. Being locked up for so long really damages your spirits. You feel forgotten.

CHAPTER FOUR

Patrick

While I was walking around Brighton with Henry in February, I was also thinking about leaving my job. Moments after Jan called me in Kabul to say that our son was in a mental hospital, I had phoned *The Independent*'s foreign editor, Leonard Doyle, to explain why I must leave Afghanistan at once and fly back to Britain. As I was speaking, he interrupted me to say that the paper, facing rising costs and inadequate revenues, had decided to close its Moscow office, where I had been a correspondent since 1999. I did not give this as much thought at the time as I would have in any other circumstances because I was completely preoccupied with Henry. I knew that even if the paper had not been closing down its Moscow operation, I would have to leave Russia because of the need to look after him. But once the initial crisis was past and Henry had agreed to take his medication, I began to feel angry with the paper for abolishing my job so soon after I had spent some highly dangerous and uncomfortable months sleeping on the floors of mud brick houses in Afghanistan on its behalf during the war against the Taliban. There was nothing personal in the

action taken by *The Independent*, which had closed two other foreign
bureaus at the same time. Leonard said there was another job available in London, though it was not clear what it would be. Alterna-
tively, I knew that I could take a redundancy package, which, after
twelve years of working on the paper, was worth considerably more
than a year's salary. This would give me the time and money to spend
my best energies helping Henry without having to work for a living.
Jan and I were hoping he would be well enough to return to Brighton Art College for the autumn term. A further unspoken motive
on my part was a vague, instinctive, but compelling feeling that if I
sacrificed, at least for a time, my journalistic career for my son, then
perhaps this sacrifice would be rewarded by his recovery.

I had not decided what to do about resigning from *The Independent* when Dr Angus told me in early March that Henry was
responding to the olanzapine. I immediately made plans to return
to Moscow to go through the tedious business of closing down the
paper's office as quickly as possible. I was not looking forward to
giving my assistant, Olga, and driver, Pavel, both of whom I liked a
lot, the dispiriting news that they were about to become unemployed.
But if I moved fast, I could be back in England by the time Henry
was well enough to leave the Priory and return to Canterbury. A
foreign correspondent's life is necessarily nomadic, and in the past I
had felt the wrench of changing the country where I lived every few
years. At least in this case, I had no choice but to go. I threw myself
into getting rid of the newspaper's two apartments – one the office
and the other where I lived – on different floors of a massive block
in south Moscow. Dealing with the Russian bureaucracy was time-
consuming and aggravating, but I found it oddly soothing because it
diverted my mind from thinking about Henry all the time. Jan found
the same thing true. Hearing of our problems, kind colleagues in her
university department offered to take over some of her lectures or

classes. She always turned them down because she found it a relief to have to think and talk about Charlotte Brontë or William Wordsworth instead of Henry's psychosis.

Even so, I thought a lot about Henry as I packed up in Moscow. I wondered how he had been affected for the worse by Jan's and my living in different countries for so much of his life. Separation had been inevitable if we were both to pursue our chosen careers. Many marriages founder because of the husband and wife working or living in different parts of the world, a common dilemma that has no obvious solution. Jan and I knew of many marriages or relationships that had collapsed or become unhappy because one person, usually the woman, had given up a job to stay with a partner. The stresses of long-distance marriages affect everybody from American bankers to Filipino nannies. In our case, the strains were even greater because as a foreign correspondent I was seldom stationary even in the city I was meant to be living in. Although I was a correspondent in Moscow for the two and a half years prior to Henry's breakdown, I spent much of my time travelling to Siberia, the Caucasus, the Caspian, or Ukraine, and I covered the wars in Chechnya and Afghanistan. Similarly, during my previous posting in Jerusalem, I had spent long weeks in Iraq, which I knew very well and had been visiting since 1977. Foreign correspondents necessarily specialise in crises and disasters, but in my case, these often took the form of wars and armed conflicts. The marriages of my friends who were foreign correspondents frequently failed to survive these prolonged and unpredictable absences. There is a camaraderie among war correspondents that tends to exclude other people, be they partners or friends. The case of the journalist who survives and flourishes in wartime but flounders when coping with domestic life is so common as to be a cliché.

I was conscious of the high casualty rate in terms of domestic happiness and life expectancy. My best friend in the 1980s was David

Blundy, a brilliant journalist whose tumultuous private life contributed to his spending his final months covering civil wars in Central
America, where he was shot dead by a rebel sniper in El Salvador
in 1989. My best friend in the 1990s was Juan-Carlos Gumucio, an
equally brave and charismatic correspondent who remained in Beirut
after other journalists had fled the city for fear of kidnapping. He had
four failed marriages behind him and was a heavy drinker verging on
alcoholism when he killed himself in his native Bolivia in 2002.

Jan and I felt these strains on our marriage, particularly after
Henry was born in 1982 and Alex in 1987. Jan felt she was undertak-
ing too much of the burden of bringing up two children and would
occasionally annoy me by referring to herself as a single mother. I
said that such mothers did not get telephoned daily by their husbands,
regardless of difficulty. I felt that I was also the loser because I lived
in lonely and dangerous places and I did not see enough of the children. In one sense, this loss was self-inflicted, but I was in my thirties
when the boys were born, and it was getting too late to change what
I did for a living. Nor did I seriously want to. These problems never
went away, but our marriage lasted, unlike those of many of my colleagues, because we were united by strong affection and we both did
jobs that we loved and gave us great satisfaction.

I had not believed that Henry and Alex suffered severely from our
separated lives, but now, in the wake of Henry's breakdown and Alex's
unhappiness at school, I was not so sure. I tried not to wallow in guilt,
which, I could see, was all too easy to do after Henry was diagnosed
with schizophrenia. Suddenly, every decision Jan and I had made about
his upbringing and education over the previous twenty years felt like an
obvious, culpable, and avoidable blunder. I kept imagining – though,
rationally, I knew it was nonsense – that had Henry gone to a boarding
school in Scotland, where my brothers and I received our secondary
education, instead of King's School in Canterbury as a day boy, all

might have been well. Perhaps in Scotland his transition from adolescence to adulthood would have been less stressful and he would have had less easy access to cannabis. But since we had no idea why Henry had schizophrenia, it made no sense to think that a different school in a different country would have helped. I knew that this retrospective wish fulfilment was not useful and that obsessively mulling over past mistakes was a waste of time, if only because there was nothing I could do about them. Even so, I could not help looking back over Henry's life, searching for signs of his present troubles and wondering if there was anything we could have done to avert them.

I remembered the day Henry was born, in the Hammersmith Hospital in London on January 4, 1982. It was exceptionally cold for southeast England, and there had been a heavy snowfall that lay thick on the ground. After watching Jan give birth – a difficult cesarean – I told her to stay in the hospital as long as she could because it was the warmest place in London. She and the infant Henry returned ten days later to my cavernous but cold and ill-maintained apartment in Paddington, where the kitchen ceiling had collapsed in a cloud of white dust three weeks before Jan went into the hospital. Henry was moved to his own room but with an intercom so we could be sure he was all right. We nervously turned the volume to maximum so Henry's shallow breaths reverberated through the whole apartment. After several weeks, Jan went to stay with my mother, Patricia, in her large house on a cliff overlooking the sea on the south coast of Ireland. My father had died there in December at the end of the previous year, and my mother was glad of the company. Three weeks later, Jan returned to Canterbury, while I was spending much of my time in Beirut waiting for the Israeli invasion of Lebanon.

When that attack finally began, I was in Syria and unable to get back to London for Henry's christening: Israeli and Syrian planes were fighting each other in the skies over Damascus, and the airport was shut. Like so many of the conflicts in the Middle East that I covered over the next thirty years, the invasion was planned as a short-term operation but turned into a lengthy and draining guerrilla war. I spent most of the next eighteen months in Lebanon, though I returned to Canterbury as often as I could.

Henry in Moscow, aged three

Ever since he learned to crawl, Henry was an enchanting child. With his blonde hair, he looked like a friendly cherub, smiling frequently, responsive to others, with a strong sense of fun and a great appetite for life. He moved from speaking single words to complete sentences with the disconcerting speed of infants. I had bought a VCR, and I liked watching operas on it. Henry, even as a very small boy, liked watching them, too, and we would sit together on cushions in front of the television watching Puccini's *La Bohème*, an opera which Henry always called "The Blue Hen." On a later occasion, when he must have been about three, I asked him: "Would you like to watch *The Barber of Seville?*"

"Yes," he said with an enthusiasm which surprised me because I did not imagine he would have heard of the opera. He plonked down beside me on a cushion and sat watching the screen with great attention. After twenty minutes, he became increasingly restless and asked in a disappointed voice, "Why aren't there any elephants?"

It turned out that he had thought he was watching an opera called "Babar of Seville" and he had been looking forward to seeing Babar, the famous French children's book fictional elephant.

In 1984, I became Moscow correspondent of *The Financial Times* and asked Jan if she could take a couple of years' unpaid leave from her university and come to live in Moscow, the first time all three of us would be together on a permanent basis. The city held an allure for her, thanks to an early passion for Tolstoy, and she also wanted time to finish her first book, on feminism and poetry. Our period in Russia worked out well from the beginning. Jan and Henry arrived in Moscow towards the end of the brief Russian summer in 1985, after I had got the apartment ready. It was in a foreigners-only building on the corner of an alleyway called Sadovaya-Samotechnaya, off the Garden Ring, a traffic-filled main road circling inner Moscow. Our apartment was relatively spacious by Soviet standards, and its main room was large and well lit. Henry liked to ride around its polished wooden parquet floor in a red Russian plastic tractor I had bought in Detsky Mir, the biggest toy shop in Moscow. Jan and I found the city well adapted to the requirements of a three-year-old. Not far from the block where we lived was a children's play area that Henry called "the horsey park" because it was filled with carefully carved wooden horses, on which he and other children liked to sit, as well as swings and seesaws. Ordinary Soviets were wary of adult foreigners but more forthcoming when faced with a cheerful three-year-old beaming up at them. In the noisy, crowded farmers' markets, gnarled peasant women liked to pinch Henry's cheeks, pat him on the head, and give him slices of apple. Our apartment block, nicknamed "Sad Sam," was heavily guarded by policemen twenty-four hours a day, and its inhabitants grumbled ceaselessly about being spied upon by the Soviets. But the advantage of this constant monitoring was that the courtyard where the children played was entirely safe. Soviet security men and staff were a little less robotlike when dealing with Henry and other small children than they were in their relations with their parents, who were mostly diplomats or journalists. Once I saw a tough-looking policeman at the entrance to Sad Sam catch Henry's attention and point silently with his hand towards his massive boot. A small mouse had taken refuge in the instep and, to Henry's delight, was nervously peering out. Another time Henry was disconsolate because he had dropped a much loved LEGO figure down a lift shaft so it lay at the bottom, tantalizingly visible but seemingly irretrievable. An ingenious maintenance worker rescued the toy by "fishing" for it with a long pole on the end of which he had put a blob of glue. This he manoeuvred to bring into contact with the LEGO piece, which stuck to it and was returned to a joyful Henry.

Henry, Jan, and Patrick   *Henry and Jan*
in Moscow, 1985

Moscow is easy enough to live in during the short spring and summer, when the trees burst into leaf and the parks are full of lilac. During these months, its climate is much the same as a Western European or North American city's. More testing is the long winter, less because of the cold than the depressing lack of light – the days are not only short but also murky – and because the sidewalks and roads are treacherous. However, Henry was highly excited by the prospect of snow in large quantities, something he had never experienced. As the days passed and winter came closer, he would look expectantly out the windows of his bedroom every morning when he woke up, hoping to see the ground carpeted with white. Finally, it happened, and Henry tore off his pyjamas, put on a pair of dark blue snow boots, and rushed naked down the staircase, intending to revel in the snow; fortunately, he was intercepted by Jan.

Henry enjoyed his school, which was called the Anglo-American and was housed in the rather dowdy buildings of what had once been a Soviet school. It had an excellent nursery school programme run on American lines, and its teachers were notably intelligent. Henry had a particularly able teacher called Jean Marie Finnerty, a tall, striking-looking American who insisted that her class visit the sights of Moscow and get to know the country they were living in. As a result, the children probably saw more of the city than their diplomatic parents, many of whom lived in a high state of paranoia and self-imposed isolation. Henry went to Red Square, of which he and the other children made a model with a small doll representing Lenin in his tomb. They visited Novodevichy Convent, with its redbrick walls rising beside a lake and an elaborate cemetery on its grounds. Ms Finnerty wrote down the rather prosaic comments of her pupils, including Henry's: "I liked the park, the arches and the slits in the wall."

In summer there were more places to go. Jan and I would take Henry to Serebryany Bor, a charming area of silver trees, small islands, and sandy beaches on the Moskva River. Journeys outside Moscow into the Russian countryside were frustratingly limited for foreigners by elaborate and rigorously enforced Soviet security rules. Closer to hand was a pretty eighteenth-century garden, created to grow medicinal herbs by Peter the Great, where we watched the ducks in a large pond shaded by ancient trees.

Henry and I always liked being together, even if we were not doing anything very interesting. Sometimes I would work at home on my typewriter, which Henry called a "typefighter," and he would stand, watching me intently. He was very sociable and got on well with other children, but he was easily cast down if they rebuffed him. I remember trying to comfort him as he sat on my knee in his bedroom at the end of a party to celebrate his fifth birthday, which was taking place in the main room. It had all gone horribly wrong for Henry, who was in floods of tears because another child had blown out one of the candles on his birthday cake before he could.

But if he was sensitive himself, he was also sensitive to the feelings of others. Once we took him to Helsinki on the overnight train from Moscow, though the trip turned into a disaster because Henry caught the flu. I bought him an American Indian feather headdress which he wore forlornly as he sat in the hotel room, engulfed by a vast double bed. I do not think he was interested in the headdress, but he kept thanking me for getting it and assuring me that it was what he had always wanted, as if it were going to make all the difference in cheering him up.

I was sorry when Jan, Henry, and Alexander, who had been born earlier that spring, went home in the summer of 1987. I knew there was no point in asking Jan to stay longer because she would have had to give up her university job. She had enjoyed Moscow and was pleased to have finished her book, but she found expatriate social life exasperating due to the de facto division between the working journalists, diplomats, and businesspeople on the one hand, and their nonworking spouses on the other. This was largely a division between men and women. Jan said, "The men talk shop and the women talk shopping." Her Moscow experience made her even more determined to keep her career and not become a full-time housewife, doomed to follow her journalistic husband from posting to posting. A final set of pictures in an old scrapbook, dated June 19, 1987, show Henry's farewell party on a beach at Serebryany Bor with balloons tied to bushes and the dark woods behind. Henry's small figure is dressed as a knight in silver armour, and he clutches a red and yellow plastic hockey stick. With Jan and the boys gone, I found the apartment empty and gloomy. I left Moscow myself six months later and, after a year in Washington, went back to England.

There was scarcely room for us all in the little house in Canterbury. Henry regarded his new brother, Alex, born the same year that he and his mother left Moscow, with wary affection, viewing him partly as an interesting new pet but also as a competitor for his parents' attention. He looked pained to see favourite toys and possessions taken over by Alex. In early 1990, when Henry was eight and Alex not yet two, Alex liked to go to sleep in his bed wearing a pink helmet from Henry's skateboard set, a yellow plastic sword from Moscow that Henry had been given as a present, and an elaborate leather and brass belt from Morocco known to the family as "the bandit's belt," which was a gift to Henry from my mother, who had obtained it when travelling in Morocco sixty years earlier. There was little friction between the two boys, but Henry's displays of affection for Alex were sometimes openly theatrical. With the sensitive emotional antennae of the very young, Alex seemed to understand his elder brother's ambivalent feelings. At about the age of four, responding to a rather ironic good-night kiss from Henry, Alex said, "Henry loves me and he doesn't like me."

Henry and Alex

Canterbury was a good place for Henry and Alex to grow up. The city is the official residence of the archbishop and the centre of the Anglican Church but little bigger than a market town, with a population of some thirty thousand. Many of its buildings date from the Middle Ages, and its narrow streets and alleys were designed for pedestrians rather than for cars or buses. The small scale was ideal for Henry, who could easily walk to and from his school and visit his friends on foot. He attended St Peter's Methodist Primary School, just inside the old city walls and overlooked by a towering medieval gateway. It was a well-run, happy school which Henry enjoyed. I used to meet him there and walk home with him along the ancient alleyways and paths of the city. For a long time his classroom was housed in a wooden cabin, as the school's plan to erect new buildings had been delayed by the discovery by construction workers of a medieval cemetery dating from the time of the Black Death. Archaeologists were slowly excavating the skeletons, and the school play-ground was bisected by deep trenches, dangerous at all times of year and full of water in winter. The children became accustomed to see-ing recently unearthed skulls peering up at them out of the diggings. They also became used to skipping blithely along rickety wooden planks bridging the trenches to reach their classrooms, while I and other parents followed gingerly behind them.

Henry flourished in Canterbury. The cathedral city had the inti-macy of a village in which his family, his friends, and his school were all close to hand. Whenever I walked down the High Street with him, we ran into people he knew every few minutes. Henry's curiosity about the wider world was expanding, and from the age of about eight, he read with real attention. He was becoming interested in everything from the solar system to plants, animals, the fate of the tropical rain forest, and the ozone layer. His quest for knowledge was typical enough for children of his age, but I felt that with Henry, there was originality and gaiety in his approach to the outside world. He enjoyed jokes and elaborate fantasies. At St Peter's School, he and his best friend, Chris, kept as pets two invisible moles – Henry's named Pekie and Chris's Moly – who had supposedly once belonged to an invisible circus but had escaped and now lived with the boys. Pekie's home was in a cupboard in Henry's bedroom. The moles accompanied Henry and Chris to school, where the boys ate their packed lunches and claimed their pets had their own invisible and much more appetizing food, such as shashlik, which was cooked for them in special ovens.

CHAPTER FIVE

Patrick

I was doing rather less well than Henry was since we came back to England. My mother died after a long and painful illness at the end of 1989. I did not enjoy working in the home office of *The Financial Times*, writing on British business, about which I knew little, after the excitement and interest of covering Moscow, Beirut, and Belfast. Canterbury was too far from London for me to commute, so I had to rent rooms from friends in London during the week. I started looking around for a new job, and *The Independent*, a recently founded and highly regarded radical newcomer to the daily press, made me its Middle East editor in the summer of 1990.

Within weeks Saddam Hussein invaded Kuwait, making Iraq, a country I knew well, the centre of an international crisis which was to continue on and off for the next two decades. I knew enough people in Baghdad to be among the first journalists to get a visa to Iraq after the Kuwait invasion. I made plans to go there. Jan was not happy about my covering the impending war, but she saw that I would be miserable if I did not go. When the bombing started and I was in Baghdad, she was very worried but was helped by the sympathy of the boys' admirable nanny, Sigal, an Israeli in Canterbury for a year, whose family was also being bombarded. Henry, though only nine when the war started, was vociferously against it from the start. His pacifism predated the invasion. On July 4, a month before Saddam Hussein's attack, he wrote an anti-war poem that he tried to persuade his teachers to allow him to read to the school assembly. In the original spelling, it went:

War is the wound of man's career
The madness wich is war
The pain
It hurts to others
It recks the homes of others
And worst of all the deaf
The anger
The feeling of it

When the war started in February the following year, Henry was worried about my safety, since I was in Baghdad, and for the people of Iraq in general. He wrote to John Major, the prime minister, denouncing the bombing and, on his own initiative, went out to the Long Market, a pedestrian precinct in Canterbury, to gather signatures in support of his letter. After a little over an hour, he returned home, justifiably proud to have collected thirty-nine signatures. He wrote another letter to Tony Benn, the anti-war politician, which never got posted but was along the same lines as his one to Major. It was eloquent, for all of the erratic spelling and punctuation:

Canterbury

tony benn
I don't now what to think of war except the two facts its not the way to
deal with things there always's another way and secondly both sides are

rong for fighting. You should never bom anyone or anything if one mans
done rong you shouldn't take the country for blame for all you now the
nicest man in the world who you are killing. And people like my dad are
the only ones who tell what's realy happening. If people thought what it
would be to be bomed yourself they would think differently.

yours sincerely
Henry Cockburn

A reply eventually came from Major or, more likely, his secretary, saying that Kuwait had been retaken with minimal loss of British lives. Henry was puzzled, saying, "But that's not what I wrote to him about." He wrote again to Major, condemning the purchase of weapons when there were people who were without houses. This time he received no reply.

In 1992, for no particularly good reason other than the quirks of office politics, *The Independent* asked me to go to Washington as one of its correspondents. I liked the city well, having worked there in the past and because my brother, Andrew, and his wife, Leslie, lived there. I bought a large house in Mount Pleasant, close to the zoo and to Rock Creek, the deep glen that runs through Washington. Jan took two years' sabbatical, and we arranged for Henry to go to Georgetown Day School and Alex to a kindergarten called Little Folks. Henry was more daunted by going to the US than I'd expected. In many ways, he was such a confident and high-spirited ten-year-old that I was caught by surprise when his morale drooped and he was intimidated by new people and new situations. On the day he left St Peter's, he wrote a sad poem of farewell that began:

I wish, I wish, I wish I could stay away,
I wish, I wish, I won't go away

It took time for the homesickness to ebb. The Washington zoo was a ten-minute walk from our house, and we often went to visit. Still regretting Canterbury, Henry wrote a poem empathizing with a depressed-looking lion he had seen in a cage:

> *I lie and watch the bars of steel and just wait for my next meal,*
> *Alas, alas, I can't go back, they won't let me back to my habitat*

Alex was less downcast by the move to Washington. Much of the time he was absorbed by a precocious interest in science and mathematics even before he could read. He insisted on learning his multiplication tables at the same time as Henry, and having moved on to Georgetown Day after a year, he would spend two hours every evening reading books about dinosaurs and a maths book from school. He liked to be read to at night from a book called *Fibonacci Numbers*. Henry occasionally showed signs of impatience at his brother's precocity. At age twelve, he vehemently announced to Jan, "It's no good, I'm not an intellectual, Mummy. You're an intellectual, Daddy's an intellectual, Alexander's an intellectual – I'm *not* an intellectual."

This was rather understating his abilities, and though he found his school hard work at first because he was a year younger than the rest of his class, he was able to keep up with the others. There was some difficulty his second year as all the other children had gone through puberty and he had not. But by now his homesickness had disappeared, he had friends his own age, and he was popular with his teachers. They liked his impish humour, cheerfulness, and high intelligence and were pleased that he read independently and wrote poetry. Georgetown Day was a particularly good school, probably the best Henry ever went to. His American teachers were skilled at making him work hard and more appreciative of his originality than their English equivalents.

When we returned to Britain after two years in America, Henry went to a school called Barton Court Grammar School on the outskirts of Canterbury. This turned out to be a bad choice. Unlike at Georgetown Day, he was a year in front of the other students and was bored by doing the same work again. In a conformist and philistine environment, Henry was different enough from the others to be singled out for bullying. His teachers were too feeble to do anything to stop it, and he feared even to bring his drawings or paintings to school, certain they would be torn up by other pupils. After a wretched year, it was clear that we would have to send him to a different place; this time the choice was King's School Canterbury, an ancient and famous public school in the precincts of the cathedral. Spurred on by his determination to get out of Barton Court, Henry took and passed the entrance examination after only a few weeks' study. He scraped through, but this was a considerable achievement, since he was competing against other students who had spent years being prepared for the same examination at expensive private schools. He celebrated the escape from his old school by heaping up all his notes from there in the backyard of the Castle Street house and setting fire to them. He carefully collected the ashes and put them in a jam jar neatly labelled BARTON COURT.

Unfortunately, he had started taking cannabis there and continued doing so after he left. At this time the British school system was awash with cheap cannabis. Going to another school would not necessarily have made much difference in its availability. He himself says he smoked it continuously from the age of fourteen, though Jan and I did not realise this. I was brought up in a heavy-drinking Irish culture, and I never took drugs like cannabis seriously. It was widely available at Oxford when I was a student there, but I probably smoked it about twice in my life. I was shocked when, in 1997, Henry did an exchange with a French student whose parents lived in the Loire Valley. We expected him to be there for several weeks, but he was back in Canterbury after a few days because, soon after his arrival, he had offered the French boy some cannabis and suggested they smoke it together. The boy told his parents, who instantly demanded that Henry end the exchange and return to England. Jan and I were upset, but we both thought cannabis was fairly harmless. It wasn't until Henry was in the hospital that we learned of its possible devastating impact on somebody genetically predisposed to schizophrenia. At the time, our main worry was that King's would hear about what had happened in France and expel Henry.

Henry in his school uniform, aged fifteen and sixteen

Henry spent five years at King's, one of Britain's leading schools, which claims with some hubris to be the oldest in the country. It is probably truer to say that there has been a school on the same site ever since St Augustine arrived in Canterbury fifteen hundred years earlier on his mission to convert the pagan Anglo-Saxons. Part of the school was housed in medieval buildings in which monks attached to the cathedral had once lived. Henry found this burden of history and tradition irksome. I sensed that he felt a little out of place amid the conformist customs of British upper-middle-class education. In cartoons he was drawing at this time, he mocked the school's not very onerous regulations and rituals, such as wearing formal black jackets and winged collars, as if students were aping the golden youth of the Edwardian era at the height of the British Empire.

Henry's teachers found him friendly, open, talented, and intellectually sharp but also irritatingly wayward, disengaged, and disorganised. They intermittently complained of his lack of the public school virtues: grit, determination, and self-discipline. On the other hand, he seemed able to pull himself together before examinations and perform better than he or his teachers expected. King's also encouraged Henry's art to a degree that had never happened before, and not only in the classroom. His designs and drawings were soon on school T-shirts, posters, and magazines.

His more carefully conceived pictures struck me as sophisticated and original. Jan, Alex, and he had been to Petra, in Jordan, where the two-thousand-year-old buildings were carved out of the red rock. On his return to Canterbury, Henry started making preparatory sketches for a larger painting that was also a political allegory. When complete, it pictured a giant apple, the sides of which had been eaten, leaving the top and bottom of the core intact. Here were pictured strange cities similar to the ruins Henry had seen in Petra, the palaces of the rich sprouting from the top of the apple and crumbling apartment blocks of the poor squashed together at the bottom. It was a surprising picture for a seventeen-year-old and won a valuable prize for local artists from Pfizer. King's was pleased but a little baffled by Henry. His very able English teacher Bill Browning wrote just before Henry left King's that "it used to be hard to track down this rather mysterious figure who, dolphin-like, popped up only every now and then," and observed that what Henry wrote was rarely up to the high standard of his conversation. But as had happened

in the past, Henry did better than he or his teachers expected, and his
A-level grades in art, English, and history were good enough to get
him into most universities in Britain.

Henry's sketch for his prizewinning
picture of an apple core

After King's, Henry went to art college in Wimbledon to do a
foundation year before going on to Brighton. I visited him there, and
he was cheerful and seemed to be having a good time. Probably I
overestimated his self-confidence because he was always more confident around me. I noticed that he did not have a girlfriend, but I did
not see what I could do about this. He also seemed peculiarly inept
at organising his own housing: he had a room the size of a coffin in a
house he shared with other students. In retrospect, I probably did not
see that Henry needed me no less as a young man of eighteen than

he had as a small boy of eight. By the time I was in my late teens, I had spent nine years mostly away from home at boarding schools, while Henry was only just leaving home for the first time. I thought it would be good for him to stand on his own feet, and I intentionally did not interfere much in his life.

At about this time, he produced one of his more striking paintings. It was large, six feet by four, and showed a dream landscape featuring an amphitheatre resembling the Colosseum, and in the background a city of large blocks and towers vaguely reminiscent of Moscow. Presiding over the amphitheatre was a beast-headed god, his head half turned away. The amphitheatre's surface was the face of a gigantic clock, with its hands being dragged around by tiny human figures. These small figures were naked and bleeding and being pursued by a devouring wolf. The meaning of the picture, produced in the summer of 2000, is not easy to understand, but it shows that Henry's artistic imagination was finding it easy to visualise a world full of dark forces and menacing demons.

CHAPTER SIX
Patrick

I called Henry every day from Moscow when he was in the Priory Hospital. I felt better for phoning him, but when I asked him how he was, he would say "I'm all right, Dad" or "Things are not too bad" in a depressed tone. I told myself that I could hardly expect him to sound cheerful, since he was shut up in a mental hospital, and I made mindlessly upbeat remarks about everything "coming right at the end of the day." I did not like leaving England while he was still ill, but I had to return to Moscow to start packing up, and it seemed a good moment at the beginning of March, after Dr Angus said he was responding to the medication.

Improvement was slow to come. Jan and Alex saw Henry on March 10 and spent a grey, gusty day walking with him around Brighton. He ate ravenously, stopping to eat fish in one place, pasta in another, and sushi in a third. During their visit, he spoke little and had a dour, abstracted look on his face. He was unshaved and dressed in clothes so dirty that one restaurant almost threw him out. Once again he complained that his art-student friends did not come to see him in the

Priory, but when they greeted him on the street, he said very little in reply before hurrying on.

A few days later, I was back in Brighton for another meeting in Henry's attic room with him, Dr Angus, Jan, and me. The subject this time was when Henry would be well enough to be released. He was desperate to get away from the hospital, with its polite staff and locked doors. I remember him standing in the middle of the floor, looking and sounding very much like a prisoner, as he pleaded to be released. "I could help at home," he said pathetically. "I could cook and help around the house."

Henry had cleaned himself up, shaved, and was wearing socks and underpants for the occasion. He gave the impression of being much more lucid and rational than a month earlier. Probably he had figured out what to say and do to convince the doctor that he was well enough to go home. We agreed that he should spend Easter in Canterbury at the end of March, and, if that went well, he would leave the Priory permanently. Signs that he was on the mend were scant, but he did not have to prove that he was cured, only that he was no danger to himself or others. Aside from overseeing his medication, the Priory staff could do little for him, and he was obviously very unhappy there. His trial visit home to Canterbury did not go entirely smoothly. It had been agreed that he should not wander off on his own, so when he disappeared out the door on the first day, I hobbled after him, shouting for him to come back. He reluctantly returned and went back to the Priory, as agreed, at the end of his visit. A few days later, I picked him up in a taxi at the Priory to bring him home, nine weeks after he slipped into the freezing water at Newhaven.

There was another reason for us to bring Henry home, though it would not have weighed with Jan and me had we thought that the hospital was doing him any good at this stage. It was the high cost of his treatment at the Priory, where he was a private patient and was not being paid for by the National Health Service (NHS). That he was in a private hospital at all was the accidental result of the fact that on the night he had been rescued at Newhaven and was diagnosed as being a danger to himself, there was no bed available in a National Health mental hospital so he was sent to the Priory. The NHS paid for his first week there, but then a bed became free in a government mental hospital in Brighton. Medical facilities there would have been as good as at the Priory, though a private room could not be guaranteed. But Jan and I were in a state of shock and turned down the NHS offer, saying we would pay for the Priory ourselves. We did this largely because of our extreme ignorance about how mental health was treated in Britain. My picture of a state mental institution was imprecise but lurid, coloured by nightmarish memories of eighteenth-century cartoons showing brutalised patients strapped to their beds or chained to the walls. These ideas were reinforced by watching patients being intimidated by authoritarian attendants in the film *One Flew Over the Cuckoo's Nest*.

At least at the Priory, we knew what we were getting, though we were paying more than we could afford. In the short term, Jan's father, Hugh Montefiore, paid a generous chunk. Marjorie Wallace, heroic campaigner for the rights of the mentally ill, warned me later against self-imposed financial ruin brought on by supposing that private treatment in Britain was superior to that provided by the state. She spoke of desperate parents or family members bankrupting themselves by paying for vastly expensive treatment for loved ones in private clinics, in pursuit of an imaginary cureall or super-drug. "Unfortunately, they don't exist," Marjorie told me. "Whatever you do, stick to the National Health Service."

Until Henry became ill, I knew little about madness: like so many other people, I found it frightening and alien. This fear must have been deep-seated in me from an early age. As a small boy growing up in the ancient town of Youghal in East County Cork in Ireland in the 1950s, I used to visit the house of my nanny, Kitty Lee, on Church Street. Opposite her home was a large grey building with PROTESTANT ASYLUM inscribed in large letters above the door. This always embarrassed me, as I had come across the word "asylum" solely in the context of "mental asylum," one of which was built on a hill overlooking Youghal and was known locally as "the mental." I knew there were few enough Protestants in our overwhelmingly Roman Catholic town, and I thought it showed the community to which I belonged in a poor light that we needed such a large building to house insane Protestants. Even if such extensive accommodation was necessary, I wished the inscription had not so brazenly advertised the fact.

In later years, my ignorance of mental illness did not significantly recede. As a student at the end of the 1960s, I was generally well read; like so many people of my generation, I had read a certain amount by Sigmund Freud and his followers but almost nothing about serious mental illness or how it was treated. Jan and I learned a lot about disorders of the mind during those first months of coping with Henry's breakdown. In the past, when people spoke of mental illness, I did not pay enough attention or have a concrete idea what they were talking about. But now I was sensitised to anything relating to mental illness and talked almost obsessively about it with anybody who mentioned it. I found it astonishing that so many people I thought I knew well turned out to have close family members suffering from schizophrenia or bipolar disorder. I wondered why they had not spoken about it to me. Even now I find their silence a little surprising, since most of them were sophisticated and self-confident, not likely to be intimidated by the "stigma" attached to anything to do with madness. They were undoubtedly inhibited, as I was occasionally to be in the years to come, by a sense that schizophrenia required too much explaining and was too serious and hurtful to be referred to fleetingly. But again and again, when I explained what had happened to Henry, people opened up about their own experiences with mental illness.

James Fox, a journalist and author, had been a friend of mine for many years, but it was only when I told him that Henry had been diagnosed with schizophrenia that I discovered he knew all too much about the disorder: his sister, Phyllis, had suffered from it for thirty years, during which he had looked after her, as their parents had died young. It was ominous and frightening that James and others I talked to at this time shared an unspoken assumption that coping with schizophrenia was a lifetime sentence and the victim never really got better. "I don't want to depress you," said James, "but after thirty years we are still dealing with the problem of how to persuade Phyllis to take medication." She did not think there was anything wrong with her and was convinced that the menacing and obscene voices she heard were real and not part of her illness.

While packing up in Moscow, I talked a lot with Pat Tyler, one of my best friends and the *New York Times* bureau chief. I had known him since the Gulf War in 1991 as a brave, sensitive, and immensely able journalist. We usually talked about Russia, America, or the war in Chechnya, but unexpectedly, we discovered we had each been hit by a mental health crisis involving a close relative. We reacted similarly and a little naively, determined to secure the right kind of doctors, medication, and medical institutions in order to cure our loved ones. Pat knew more than I did because this was the second time a member of his family had been diagnosed with a mental disorder: his elder brother, Mike, with whom he was very close, had bipolar disorder and was schizoid-affective, which means showing at least some symptoms of schizophrenia. I found it dispiriting that nobody was speaking about cures, but at least afflicted people seemed able to live some sort of normal life.

I spent April and May partly in Canterbury with the family when I was not wrapping up unfinished business at *The Independent*. I was not entirely sure I was doing the right thing in leaving the paper, but I felt that if there was anything I could do to help Henry get better, I should do it now. Jan and I had been told that it was very important for him not to have more than one schizophrenic breakdown, that if there was only one, the chances of his resuming a normal life were good. This seemed possible, since Henry's new consultant doctor in Canterbury said optimistically that we could aim at seeing our son go back to his art college in Brighton the next academic year, starting in October. In retrospect, leaving my job was probably a mistake, though I could not have known at the time. I had not realised that the timescale for any improvement in schizophrenia or other mental illness is likely to be far longer than a single summer. My reasoning would have made sense only if Henry had been suffering from a physical ailment such as a bad fracture or hepatitis. I also underestimated the stress of being without a job at a moment when the burden of looking after Henry was already stressful enough. Having given up *The Independent*, I obviously had less work to do, but then work could be a useful mental diversion in such circumstances.

I spent the summer trying to help Henry. I had a recurring fantasy that he and I would rent a barge and sail the canals of England, and as we did so, he would get well. More immediately, an obvious therapy was to get him painting and drawing again. Jan had a friend in Canterbury whose late husband had been a painter and had an unused studio. Henry started painting there, mostly stylised graphics, all very dark and chaotic. He chose to paint not on canvases but on old planks, sometimes with nails sticking out, but he did not produce much, and his heart was clearly not in it. He preferred singing improvised raps. I thought he might be better motivated to paint and draw if he had tuition. Under a tutor he liked, Henry did some good charcoal and pencil sketches. None of these survived because Henry was developing a habit of spontaneously giving his drawings away to whoever had been his model at the moment.

As well as trying to get Henry interested in art again, I thought it might help to put bad memories behind him if we travelled abroad, but our journeys never seemed to be as lighthearted or stress-free as I hoped. In June, Jan, Henry, Alex, and I went to Rome. I had pictured us having languid lunches with friends, but our airline lost all our suitcases, one of which included my address book, so I could not contact the friends. Henry did some excellent sketches of the Trevi Fountain and sculpture in churches, but he did not recover his old joie de vivre or mischievous sense of humour. Henry and I went to Paris, where we watched the elegant floats of a gay parade. This was enjoyable, though the police closed down the city centre for the parade and we had to walk miles back to our hotel. Probably I was overeager in trying to rekindle Henry's interest in art. We visited the Tate Modern in London to see an Impressionist exhibition, and Henry stood on the gallery's terrace, staring abstractedly and a little gloomily across the Thames towards St Paul's Cathedral.

I was never sure if I should try to shield Henry from bad news. Of my journalist friends, the one with whom Henry got on best was Juan-Carlos Gumucio, or JC as he was known. His eyes sparkling with humour, intelligence, and mischief, he was a man of Falstaffian charm and love of life who adored Henry and Alex. As a journalist,

he was full of resources: during the war in Kosovo in 1999, journalists from all over the world were trying every ploy to enter Serbia,
which was refusing to issue visas to any of them. When they finally
did persuade the Serbian authorities to let them cross the frontier,
they found to their intense irritation that they had been preceded
to Belgrade by JC in the guise of a visiting professor from Bolivia,
come to show the Bolivian people's solidarity with the Serbs in their
time of need.

Henry had seen a lot of JC in London, where he had moved in the
late 1990s, and sometimes stayed in his apartment. JC was not happy
there, as English politics bored him, and he was drinking too much,
even by his previous gargantuan standards. I once found a touching
to-do list of Henry's, which must have been written when he was
seventeen, in which one item was "tell JC not to drink so much." The
advice was disregarded, as was that of four ex-wives, numerous edi-
tors, and many friends. JC declined into dependence on alcohol and
cocaine, lost his job, and returned to Bolivia.

I was walking in Brighton in February in the rain, having spent
the day with Henry, when I got a telephone call telling me Juan-
Carlos was dead. I learned that he had shot himself with a rifle while
lying drunk beside a swimming pool at the house where he was living in Bolivia. I hesitated for several weeks before telling Henry, but
I was worried he would find out by accident. We both went to the
crowded memorial service in a church in central London on July
3 and met with his friends afterwards. Henry said that he felt he
had not done enough to save JC by steering him away from drink
and drugs. At first I thought this was rather touching, but excessive
and irrational guilt seemed to be part of Henry's illness, and for the
next few years he kept telling me that he blamed himself for the death
of Juan-Carlos.

Not all my expeditions with Henry were doleful. We went to a music festival in Belfast where I had once lived at the height of the Troubles from 1972 to 1975. The main feature of the festival was African music, which Henry enjoyed. We drove the length of Ireland to stay at the house that had once been my parents', in the village of Ardmore in County Waterford on the south coast. On the way, we stopped to look at the enormous Stone Age monuments and passage graves at Newgrange, outside Dublin. Henry dived into an underground tunnel to emerge cheerfully some distance away. He said he felt safer underground.

We spent most of August in Ardmore with Jan and Alex. Here Henry was at his best, rowing a dinghy in the calm waters of the bay. Jan took him for long walks along the top of the high cliffs around the house. He talked to her more than he did to me about his state of mind, saying to her that he thought he was a shaman, asking, "Don't you think I can do magic?" Once he jumped over a fence and stood on the edge of the cliff, looking down at the rocks below as if he intended to jump. Jan did not tell me this at the time, but when I suggested that Henry stay on with me in Ireland, where I was writing the synopsis for a book, she thought anxiously about those high cliffs and took him back to Canterbury.

The plan was for Henry to start his art courses again in Brighton. This was what he himself said he wanted to do, and Brighton University, part of his art college, would take him back, asking only that he clean up his old room, one wall of which he had covered with a messy half-finished cartoon. Jan and I were a little uncertain about his state of mind, and we suspected he was not taking his medication all the time, which was scarcely surprising, as he did not believe he was ill. In retrospect, strenuous, repetitive, but stress-free work might have been better adapted to Henry's state of mental health than a reintroduction into the unstructured bohemian world of an art student. Back in Canterbury, Henry took a job

picking hops, a plant used in making beer, work he said he found
boring and exhausting, but Jan felt that it made him happier than he
had been all summer. A streaming cold ended Henry's hop picking,
after which his mental condition became worse and he was more
and more reluctant to take his olanzapine. The date of his return
to Brighton was coming closer, and Jan and I did not know what
to do with him other than take him back there. We were also both
completely exhausted by worrying about him and making sure he
took his medication.

On the morning Henry was to return to Brighton, he suddenly
said he did not want to go back. Jan persuaded him at least to look
at his new room and see how he felt. They walked on the seashore,
and Henry said he would "like to live off the land." Later, after he
met some friends, his mood became more positive, and he told Jan,
"Thank you for making me come back here." Over the next couple
of months, Jan and I visited him often, she from Canterbury and
I from London because I do not drive and could get to Brighton
easily by train from there. Almost at once I could see he was not
getting better. I would meet him in his small dark room, and we
would wander the streets or go to his favourite café. He was not
doing much painting or drawing, and once he disappeared overnight, which he spent in a shelter for the homeless. He came back
badly scratched, as if he had been pushing his way through bushes,
and he had lost his shoes, trousers, keys, and bank card. I saw that
the students he shared his apartment with had left an impatient message in block capitals in the kitchen: HENRY PLEASE WASH UP YOUR
DIRTY PLATES IN THE SINK. He stopped shaving or washing his hair
and went barefoot, so his feet got septic and he had to go several
times to the outpatients' section of the hospital to get antibiotics. He
also soiled his jeans more than once and exhibited growing signs of
infantilism, which I knew was one symptom of his psychosis. His

dirtiness became impossible to miss. Once he met me at Brighton station wearing very grubby trousers, a jumper, sneakers, and no socks and said he had just been questioned by the police because of his appearance. He admitted to me that he was scarcely taking his medication, and I wrote despairingly to his social worker and the consultant in Brighton, asking if they could give him the olanzapine through fortnightly injections, as I knew could be done; otherwise, I feared a relapse was inevitable.

Henry came home for Christmas and briefly rallied. He was more relaxed with our family and spent time with friends back from college. His consultant in Brighton had persuaded him to take his medication during his final weeks there, and he generally went on doing this, though not at the prescribed dosage. This had been set at 10 mg in November, but he insisted that he would take only 7.5 mg. The signs of his mental disorder were evident only part of the time. People who telephoned Henry over the coming years, even when he was in a locked ward in a mental hospital, would say to me in genuine surprise how they had enjoyed an amusing and entirely rational conversation with him. On our walks, he could be sweet-natured as well as remote and abstracted.

I had expected him to go back to Brighton for his second term after his birthday on January 4 and had timed a stint at a think tank in Washington to coincide. But within a day of my leaving, Henry began to have a breakdown that Jan, heroically, dealt with alone. The evening of the day I left, he had gone off for a walk with his closest friend, a gentle hippyish young man called Peter, and did not return for a full day and night. Jan, frantic with worry, phoned everybody who might know where Henry could be. Finally, she reached Peter, who said he would take her to see Henry, who was undergoing a mystical experience. They found him sitting under a hedge in an old quarry at a place called Lime Kiln Road on the outskirts of

Canterbury. It was drizzling and the grass was very wet, but Henry insisted on staying until it was dark. He declared he was not going back to Brighton, and when Jan agreed, he walked home with her. He had soiled his trousers, and when they were back at home, he threw them out the window.

His condition continued to worsen over the following week, and Jan wrote a lengthy letter to Henry's doctor in Canterbury describing his deterioration in detail: "He won't use a key to the house," she wrote. "He insists on getting in by climbing over the wall at the back of our backyard and in by the back door, which isn't locked. He won't eat anything but vegan food, and a narrowing range of that: no rice, no potatoes, no dried fruit. He won't help prepare it – he doesn't like seeing vegetables chopped up. He tends to scatter bread crusts, nutshells and rinds around the house, as if he wants to create mess, though he does pick these up if requested and likewise small jobs like laying the table. He doesn't like using the toilet and prefers to urinate out of doors if possible (I've asked him not to do this in our yard and he has agreed). He does take baths but his feet are always dirty and sore because he doesn't wear socks, and his toenails are getting overgrown and once again he needs antibiotics for infected blisters."

The end came quickly. At about eight A.M. on January 22, almost exactly a year since Henry had first seen the golden Buddha on Brighton Beach, he left the house on Castle Street. Jan was making some tomato sauce for pasta, which was one of the few things Henry would still eat; he had not noticed that tortellini contains cheese and eggs. Jan was stirring the sauce when there was a loud knock on the door and a policeman appeared. He said, "Do you have a son called Henry Cockburn?"

"Yes."

"Well, he's been standing naked in your neighbour's garden for

twenty minutes, and she's reported him to us. Now, that is an indict-
able offence, and we could charge him with indecent exposure, only
we think he might have a mental health problem."

"You're right, he does. And what's more, he's not been taking his
medication."

"We can either let him go, or if you think it's more appropriate,
we can take him to a safe place."

"Does 'a safe place' mean a mental hospital?"

"Yes, it does."

For about twenty seconds, Jan agonised over what to do before
agreeing. Later, she got a telephone call from St Martin's, an NHS
mental hospital on extensive grounds on the outskirts of Canterbury,
which we had often driven past but had never paid much attention
to. The hospital asked for formal consent to Henry's sectioning or
legal restraint. Jan agreed, a momentous decision for Henry, but she
felt that she had already made the crucial choice about his future
when she told the policeman to take him to a mental hospital and
not release him. She went to St Martin's to bring him some clothes
and discovered he was in Anselm, a locked but not a secure ward, a
significant distinction we were to learn about later. Henry refused to
talk to or even look at her, the nurses, or the doctors. For the whole
two hours she was with him, he paced up and down his room and said
nothing to her and throughout appeared preoccupied and agitated.
Finally, she gave up waiting for him to speak and returned home.
This obsessive walking went on day and night for two or three days,
during which Henry would not eat or drink. In the end, the hospital
staff, feeling they had no choice, forcibly gave Henry an injection to
sedate him, and finally he slept.

Henry was to stay in Anselm ward for six months. For the first
two months, he refused to speak to his mother, obviously blam-
ing her for sectioning him. Then one day in the spring, he relented

and was allowed by the hospital to go with us around the grounds. These were surprisingly beautiful and included a stately circle of Scots pine trees and an overgrown pond full of small green frogs. Wildlife was abundant because rabbits, squirrels, moles, and foxes had discovered that human hunters were wary of entering a mental hospital's grounds. Henry seemed to be more stable and sometimes came home during the day. But his psychosis could suddenly return without warning.

One evening he asked Alex, now sixteen, to walk back with him to the hospital. The journey took a long time because Henry often stood still and seemed uncertain where he was going. He stopped by a brick wall and climbed on top of it and told Alex to follow, which, full of misgivings, he did. He found that Henry had jumped down into somebody's back garden, where the two of them were sheltered by a few trees. Alex suspected that Henry had been there before and was nervous that the owner of the house would discover them. He kept urging Henry to go back to the hospital, but by now he did not think that his brother, who was growing more agitated and talking to himself, could even hear him. As Henry's condition grew worse, he appeared absolutely terrified and started crying with fear. He stripped off his clothes and defecated in front of Alex, who was urging him to get dressed and leave the back garden, though he could see that Henry was too agitated to do so. Alex, despite his own great distress, behaved with great courage and determination and stayed with his brother, waiting for him to calm down. All the while Alex was wondering how the owner of the house would react if he found two strange young men in his back garden, one of them naked. It was, Alex later confessed, the worst experience of his life. After some time, Henry did become calmer, and Alex persuaded him to put his clothes back on and return to the hospital.

By now Henry was so shaky and exhausted that Alex had to put his arm round him to support him.

Perhaps unaware of the severity of such episodes, Henry's doctors felt he was getting better and sent him for the second half of the year to a halfway house at Ramsgate, a down-at-the-heel holiday resort overlooking the English Channel.

CHAPTER SEVEN

Henry

When I left the Priory to return home, nobody said good-bye. I had felt leaving was going to be more exciting. I spent the morning playing my drums, but I did not feel liberated as I stood outside the clinic with my father, waiting for a taxi to pick us up. We drove straight to Canterbury, and I was glad to be home, but I missed Brighton and the people there. I felt at a loss and didn't know what to do with myself. I had to go to the psychiatrist every week, and I was not having the same experience of being guided by the wind or talking to the trees. These visions had become the centre of my world. My parents were always urging me to draw, but I didn't want to draw, I wanted to make music. I rearranged my room in the house and bought a record player. I put cushions all around the sides of the room and wanted my friends to come and sit in the room so we could jam. This almost happened when my friends Jules and Luke came, but we spent all our time smoking dope.

I got a job in a bookshop called the Albion. They didn't pay me, and I wasn't particularly good at stacking shelves, but it passed the time. Once I went back to Brighton to re-enroll in my course for the next year. They told me I had to clean up my bedroom, which looked like a scrap heap. I had drawn all over the walls and had to repaint them. I kept going to a hardware shop to get white paint, and I used sandpaper to scratch away what I had drawn. I could hear Kitty, my dad's nanny, saying "no" every time I painted over what I had drawn on the walls, but I did it all the same.

My father took me travelling in the summer. I went to Rome, which I did not like as much as Venice. We visited Paris, where we saw a gay parade, lunched several times with my father's friend Charlie Glass, and in the courtyard of the Louvre, had the most expensive beer I have ever drunk. We went to Belfast, where I liked the African music they were playing at a festival on the Falls Road. We were travelling on a train from Brighton to London when my dad first told me that Juan-Carlos was dead. I asked when he had died and it seemed to me that I was playing bongo drums at that moment and had felt his spirit come to me in the room. I told the spirit to go back to Bolivia and start a revolution there. I blamed myself for not stopping him from taking so much cocaine and alcohol. I remembered the first time I met him was in a café in West Jerusalem when I was thirteen. I was on a search for a Zippo lighter, which I thought would be the coolest thing ever. I had looked all over Jerusalem for the lighter, but they were all either the wrong shape or too expensive. My dad and I met Juan-Carlos upstairs in a kosher restaurant. He arrived late, but we began talking – about languages, of which he could speak five, including English, Spanish, Italian, and one I have forgotten. I told him I had been looking for a Zippo, and he immediately produced a gold one from his pocket and lit a cigarette. "You can have this one," he said, and etched the letters FF on the side of the lighter with a metal pen. "That means 'friends forever,'" he said. I went to his memorial service in London, and I wanted to cry but couldn't.

Back in Canterbury, I went hops picking, which meant I had to get up early in the morning and follow a tractor hour after hour. It was very hard work, and it felt as if the day would never end, but I was paid and I bought Alex a guitar. I did not really want to go back to art college in Brighton because I was less and less interested in art. When I did return, I often felt paranoid: I believed I was being followed by white-and-green taxis, though these are common in the city. My flatmates weren't the same as a year earlier. I stopped taking my medication regularly, and I went for long walks. One day I felt the wind ushering me towards the undergrowth near the railway line. At first I said to myself, "I'm too weak. I'm not strong enough." But I did go and hide in the brambles near an abandoned building. I remember the brambles saying, "We are the gods." "Should I lie?" I asked. "Never lie, Henry," they replied. All of a sudden a woman sat down next to me. She didn't see me at first, and when she did, she gave a terrible shriek. Maybe she thought I was dead. I got up, bewildered and feeling exposed, but she was nowhere to be seen. I jumped down the side of an abandoned bridge and sat there arranging small stones. I heard a woman calling me, and I walked under the bridge, where there was a group of homeless people. There was an assortment of mattresses and salvaged chairs, as well as the woman, who turned out to be called Jackie, and two men, one named Tommy Lee, who was her boyfriend, and a big fellow called Sean. "He's the boss," said Tommy Lee. Jackie was smoking roll-ups that she kept in a tin box. She looked at me and said, "Your name is Daniel." I went along with this, though the brambles had told me not to lie. I told her I was an art student. She asked me if I wanted to paint under the bridge, but I wouldn't.

We sat there for some time until Jackie said she could see some police coming towards the bridge. Sean ran off, but I stayed where I was, though I was scared I would be taken to the police station. One of the policemen asked my name, and I stammered that it was Daniel. "Come on, kid, I wasn't born yesterday," said one of them, and I gave my real name. "Your eyes are dilated," said one of the officers, "have you been on drugs?" "Olanzapine," I answered. A policeman spelled out my last name slowly over his radio – "Charlie, Oscar, Charlie, Kilo" – but they had no record of it. "Stay safe," said one of the police, and they left. Jackie told me and a big grizzly Irishman to go and collect some wood. We walked along the side of an abandoned building, and he asked me where I was from. I told him Canterbury, and he said he knew somebody who was raped in Canterbury. We got to a track, where I picked up a big and enormously heavy piece of wood. I struggled to carry it and finally got it to the fireplace.

Jackie found an old torn-up book and started the fire. Sean, who had run off and hid, returned with somebody called Woody. Though the others were talkative, I sat away from the fire because I didn't know what to say. Sean and Woody lit a spliff with the best-smelling hash I have ever smelt. They talked and they drank, and I felt I had run into a close-knit gang of people who knew one another very well and did not know me at all. They seemed to resent my silence. Suddenly, Woody turned to me and asked, "Have you got any speed or ketamine?" I told him, "No, I'm useless." "What's your name?" "Daniel." Sean got up, looked at me, and said, "I'm going to hit him with a brick." Jackie, who had been sticking up for me all night, said, "Yeah." Sean moved towards me with a brick in his hand, and I ran out from under the bridge and hid in the bushes. When dawn came, I crept back to the bridge to collect my shoes that I'd left there and found them all asleep.

I left Brighton before Christmas, and my mother took me back to Canterbury. I told my parents that I wanted to break with family tradition and not go to Ireland for Christmas. The next day I walked into Canterbury, went to an estate, and climbed over some of the buildings there where I got soaking wet. I went to buy some tobacco and ran into my friend Luke. "Henry, you look like a prophet," he said, staring at me with my shaggy beard and wet clothes. When we next met, he was buying presents for his girlfriend in Bloomsbury. We talked about Virginia Woolf and how she had gone mad, and he said the line was thin between creative genius and insanity. Looking at me, he said, "It is as if you're permanently tripping." I have never tried acid, but I knew what he meant.

The days before I got sectioned were filled with quarrels between my mother and me. I would go for long walks around Canterbury, and she was obviously worried. On the day I was sectioned, I got up early and climbed over a neighbour's fence and into a garden. I thought the leaves of ivy brushing against my skin were telling me to pull down my trousers. The man whose house it was came into his garden for a cigarette and must have seen me, because five minutes later, the police came. They were going to let me off with a caution, but my mother told them I was schizophrenic and needed to be hospitalised. I refused to speak to her for two months. Most people would see going into the hospital as an enormous blow, and I was frightened they'd put me in a straitjacket when I first went there. At the same time I was sort of expecting to be sectioned. I had this rap song by the Roots that I kept on repeating to myself. It sounded like this:

My complexion
Section
Brother in I suffer in
Ejects I.

I was taken to the hospital in a police van. I closed my eyes, and when I opened them, I found myself in the hospital. I didn't know where I was geographically. I walked round and round the table for a good two hours, thinking that my shoes were talking to me. I remember the sound of my shoes slapping against the floor. My mum came to visit, but I didn't speak a word to her because I blamed her for putting me in the hospital.

I refused my medication for the first three days, so they forcibly gave it to me. I remember sitting there with my eyes closed while they tried to talk me into having the medication. One of them twisted my arm and made me take my medication. It was the first time I had been sectioned, and it took a while for me to find my bearings. I remember a girl called Tanya telling me not to come round her end of the hospital. That night it took me a long while to get to sleep. When I woke up, I found myself under my Peruvian rug with my special stone that somebody had given me in college lying next to me. My best friend, Peter, must have come during the night to find me asleep and had wrapped the rug around me. The next day he came round again and persuaded me to take the pills, as it was the only way I could get any fresh air.

The door to Anselm was locked, but you could ask the staff to let you out. A typical day consisted of breakfast, which I usually didn't have because I didn't wake up early enough. There was medication, which in my case meant olanzapine. Then I would walk round and round the yard for hours until it was dinnertime at five. Every week there would be a ward round when the doctor would see how you were doing.

At this point I had gone completely vegan and wouldn't eat rice or potatoes, either. Yet I would always look forward to lunch and dinner and I had lots of nut roasts, the vegetarian equivalent of roast meat. I had given up drinking, marijuana, and tobacco. Also, I wouldn't have a haircut, and my hair got matted into dreadlocks. On the outside, Anselm was overlooked by a big fence with brambles growing in it. Inside, it had a smoking room where Malcolm, one of the other patients, would smoke his pipe. Because of my Peruvian blanket, mostly yellow but with bright stripes, Malcolm called me "the man with the Technicolour dreamcoat."

Eventually, I was allowed out of Anselm with a nurse called Franchetti. The weather was so beautiful. I felt liberated. It wasn't long before I got permission to go out by myself. I saw the army barracks on the other side of the road, which I knew before, so I could see where the hospital was in relation to Canterbury. The winter passed quickly, and I remember the day spring arrived. I went to a swamp near the hospital. I looked at my reflection in a pool of water, and I saw myself in years to come with a girl I fancied. I walked round the hospital grounds jumping for joy. I could see all the buds coming out. I sang as I walked around the hospital: "It's spring, it's spring." At the time I had decided I would not cross any bridges – I thought it was crossing the river's path, in the same way that you don't want to cross certain people's paths. This meant I could go only to the east of Canterbury, as there is a river dividing the east and west parts of the city.

Being in the hospital is harrowing, particularly at first. You can't go out at night, and your leave is dependent on what the doctor thinks of your mental state. In all the time I was in Anselm, which was about six months, I did not have a single ride in a car. I didn't want to use telephones, though I can't remember why.

When I was in the acute ward, I found a metal bin and turned it upside down and used it as a drum. I thought the bins were purposely made in Zimbabwe to be used like this. I could see images flash into my mind when I played the drum. I made friends with a man called Ken. We sat in his room and played Bob Dylan's "Subterranean Homesick Blues" over and over again. We ate raw garlic and ginger. I met many people in Anselm, including two whom I knew already: Toby, one of my old dope-smoking friends, and Sean, whom I knew through a friend's father. Sean was strongly Christian. One day he wrote me a little note. It said, "Use the Lord as your strength and your shield." I said, "Aaah," as if to say "How sweet." He didn't like me saying that.

My friend Toby and I used to play hacky sack, a game involving a small ball filled with beans like a juggling ball. The aim of the game is to keep the ball in the air by kicking it with your feet. I walked into town with Toby, and we sat in the Dane John Gardens doing some rap, with me rapping and him beat-boxing (making the rhythm). He was scared people didn't like it and were laughing at us. I told him, "They liked it." He was tall, blond, well built, about nineteen at this time, and said to be a heavy user of drugs. Once he told me he was going to take a lot of heroin.

One night I came back from walking in Canterbury and was called into the office in Anselm. I was scared they were going to bust me because I had been concealing my medication and spitting it out. It turned out that something much worse had happened. Toby had committed suicide by jumping in front of a train. This surprised everyone in the ward. One of the patients rang up Toby's parents to say that he might not be dead. Toby's mother said she had seen the body and he was quite dead. The last time my mother had come to see me, I had been playing football with Toby in the garden, but now I stopped playing football.

CHAPTER EIGHT
Patrick

Henry might have died like his friend Toby during any of his disappearances or nighttime wanderings through Brighton and the countryside around Canterbury. He did not completely lose his instinct for self-preservation and occasionally sought the help of others, but his survival in the face of so many dangers was largely a matter of luck. I learned later that not everybody who had been admitted to the Priory in Hove, where he had first been taken, had been so lucky.

In February 2001, a year before Henry was there, a young guitarist named Desmond King, aged twenty-six, who was in the grip of a strong psychosis, also had a bed in the hospital. He had been brought there by his father, a tough and energetic retired Irish businessman with the same name as his son, who was convinced that his son would not receive satisfactory treatment at their local National Health hospital. His father supposed his son would be safe in the Priory, behind two sets of locked doors. Five nights later, he received an unexpected telephone call from another hospital in Brighton, the Royal Sussex, saying they had his son, who had been in an accident. "I was totally shocked," says his father. It turned out that the younger Desmond had gotten out of the Priory. "When I got to the hospital, I was told by the surgeon that it was unlikely that Desmond would survive his massive head injury . . . all his bones were broken down his right side, and both his lungs had collapsed. He was put on a life support machine, but he was not expected to come round. We found out later that he had jumped from the roof of Hove [multistory] car park."

Fortunately, he was to survive his severe injuries, though he had to endure frequent operations and long months in the hospital. His father, whose courage and determination to help his son I came to admire deeply, was soon to suffer a further calamity. "One morning," he recalls, "the phone rang at home as I was getting ready to go to the hospital, and it was my brother-in-law. He said, 'I'm really sorry, but he is dead!' I sat down on the floor and cried and asked him how he knew Desmond was in the hospital, and it turned out he did not know: He was telling me that my eldest son had died in a motorcycle accident in Smithfield, London."

This terrible story illustrates the physical perils stemming from mental disorder that threaten anybody suffering from schizophrenia. Many die young. I wanted Henry to get better, but I knew that to do so, he would have to survive self-inflicted dangers, and Jan and I did not think he would do that unless he was legally prevented from leaving whatever hospital he was in. However, he was less safe there than we hoped, and he was to disappear many times despite locked doors and high fences. Fear for his life and a belief that it was only in the hospital that he would get treatment for his disorder were our main reasons for agreeing that he should be legally confined under Section 3 of the Mental Health Act. Grim statistics, mostly from the US but also, to a lesser extent, from Britain, showed what was likely to happen if he was not protected. Of young Americans diagnosed with schizophrenia, some 10 to 13 per cent die, mostly by suicide, within

ten years of their diagnosis. In addition to those who succeed in killing themselves, some 40 per cent of men and women schizophrenics
attempt suicide at least once, the percentage for males alone rising
to 60 per cent. Henry himself says that several times he thought of
killing himself and once even wrote a suicide note. Even if suicide
was not his intention, he did very dangerous things, such as climbing
high buildings, walking near railway tracks, swimming in ice-cold
water, or running naked through the snow, any of which might have
led to his death.

People with schizophrenia are periodically demonised as potentially violent by television and newspapers, but the sad reality is that
their violence is directed mostly towards themselves. The high suicide rate is only the most visible peak towering over a mountain of
pain. "While schizophrenia is by no means the most common mental
illness," a report from the National Institute of Mental Health in the
US recorded in 1986, "it is probably the most devastating in terms
of human suffering." Unfortunately, this remains as true now as it
was then. The suffering is so great because for many, schizophrenia
is a lifetime sentence preventing them from holding a job and often
reducing them to poverty on the margins of society. The mentally ill
are not only feared but deemed, consciously or unconsciously, as not
human in the fullest sense. Dehumanisation opens the door to cruelty
and disregard by the rest of society. Of the six hundred thousand
homeless living rough on the streets or in shelters in the US, fully
one third have schizophrenia or bipolar disorder. In jails in America,
as many as a fifth of the 2.1 million prisoners have a mental illness,
and most of these have been incarcerated for minor crimes such as
trespassing. A slightly smaller number of schizophrenics are in hospitals than in shelters or jails, though many bounce miserably among
these three places.

As I previously mentioned, I was surprised to discover that so many of my friends had close relatives with schizophrenia. Though I initially suspected that the stigma of mental illness was the reason for their silence, I later saw that there was another explanation. The illness had inflicted such pain on them and their families that they did not want to talk about the details or expose them to public view even decades later. One of those I had told of Henry's schizophrenia soon after it was diagnosed was a journalist of the highest calibre and a friend for many years. A highly sympathetic and intelligent man, he told me about the dreadful fate of his sister-in-law, who was a talented woman but suffered from severe mental illness. Unfortunately, she was receiving psychotherapy from a pupil of R. D. Laing, the controversial Scottish psychiatrist who had the virtue of listening to what his patients told him but argued that parental persecution was an important factor in provoking schizophrenia and that madness itself was a creative experience. She tried to battle through a severe psychosis – in other words, a prolonged bout of madness – without being hospitalised. One day in 1973, she poured petrol over herself and lit it, badly burning over three quarters of her body. It took her weeks to die in agony. My journalist friend saw Laing and his acolytes as being at least partly to blame.

This story made me even more wary of people who suggested that Henry might survive without medication. Writing this book, I asked my friend if I could repeat his account of his sister-in-law's death. Although the event took place almost forty years ago, the wound was still too raw, and he said he would prefer the identities of those involved to be concealed. He told me, however, that a full and accurate account of the tragedy, entitled *Anna*, had been written by his brother in the form of a novel under the pseudonym David Reed. Based on his brother's diaries, it remains one of the most detailed and moving accounts I've seen of the madness of an individual and its impact on a family.

In most countries, the majority of the mentally ill are ill tended, poor, and without health insurance. Aside from people who have suffered a breakdown, most of those receiving professional psychological help are well-to-do. It is as if, on the battlefield of mental health, the psychiatrists and psychologists will treat only lightly wounded members of the officer class, and the majority of casualties are disregarded as untreatable. Dr John A. Talbot, a former president of the American Psychiatric Association, admitted that psychiatry is "one of the few specialties where the most skilled practitioners take care of the least impaired patients." Though 1.1 per cent of the world's population is estimated to have schizophrenia, limited funds are spent on research by governments. In the US, HIV (including AIDS) research receives $2,241 per person affected, compared to just $75 per person affected by schizophrenia.

I was struck by the big difference between attitudes to mental and physical illness. The dire effects of polio, about which I knew a lot, were well publicised. I caught the virus at the age of six in 1956, during what was to be almost the last epidemic to hit Western Europe, one year after an effective vaccine had been introduced by Dr Jonas Salk in the US. People were frightened by polio because it threatened their children to a degree that today is matched only by AIDS, but they were certainly not scared of people crippled by the disease, the most celebrated example being President Franklin D. Roosevelt. Contrast this with the impact on a politician who has the slightest hint of mental ill health. In the 1972 US presidential election, the revelation that Senator Thomas Eagleton had received electric shock treatment and had once checked himself into a hospital because of psychological problems was enough to get him sacked as the Democratic vice presidential candidate.

In raising money for polio research, the March of Dimes posters showed polio victims in their wheelchairs or on crutches in the correct expectation that their plight would provoke sympathy and contributions. The research was so heavily funded by the late 1940s that Dr Salk started his successful search for a vaccine, since it was the best way to get the money to keep his laboratory open. When it was announced that his serum had been successfully tested in 1955, church bells rang out in celebration across America. By comparison, the sight of victims of schizophrenia, insofar as they are ever seen, generally elicits fear and revulsion. The stereotypical mentally ill person is a raggedly dressed man or woman muttering to him- or herself, pushing a supermarket cart loaded with old clothes and plastic bags along the sidewalk. In the UK, more than one in three people think that those with schizophrenia will be violent, according to an opinion poll by YouGov. In reports on television news and in films, the typical schizophrenic often comes across as a Jekyll-and-Hyde figure, outwardly harmless and normal but in reality dangerous and mad.

Fear of mental illness has fostered public ignorance. But parallel to this is the experts' own continuing lack of understanding about what goes on in the brain to produce mental illness. Ironically, doctors often noted that Henry had lack of insight into his disorder, which meant that he did not acknowledge there was anything wrong with him. But the insight of the professionals was also limited. Over the last century, psychiatrists and psychologists have proved singularly unsuccessful in finding either causes or cures for mental disorders. Their failure is all the more glaring compared to the great advances in physical medicine, which, in a relatively short period, has seen past killers like cholera, typhus, TB, malaria, and yellow fever either eliminated or controlled. Polio has all but disappeared, and the cure for leprosy is known. Cancer is no longer the killer it once was. But treatment of mental illness boasts few such victories. The most important success was the accidental discovery in the 1950s of anti-psychotic drugs, also called neuroleptics, which reduce but do not eliminate some of the worst symptoms of schizophrenia and other mental conditions. The traditional explanation of why these drugs work – though they do not always do so – is that they reduce an excess of dopamine in the brain. But the mechanism through which the most dramatic psychotic symptoms can be reduced remains elusive. A newer generation of drugs, the so-called atypical anti-psychotics, is not necessarily proving more effective than their pre-decessors, according to recent trials, though their side effects are less debilitating. The long-term effectiveness of any kind of medication is severely undermined because at least 50 per cent of people with schizophrenia stop taking it after leaving the hospital, and 20 per cent stop while they are still hospitalised.

Possibly because of frustration by the lack of real progress, the treatment of mental health has also seen a frightening num-ber of false breakthroughs and dangerous fads, often of great barbarity, such as prefrontal lobotomy, introduced by the Portu-guese surgeon Egas Moniz in the 1930s. This crude brain opera-tion was widely practised and consisted of smashing into the front of the brain above the eyes with an instrument like an ice pick. Its most enthusiastic practitioner in the US, the neurosurgeon Dr Walter Freeman, used to drive from hospital to hospital carrying out numerous operations in a morning. So dissatisfied was one vic-tim of Moniz's pioneering operation that he shot and wounded the Nobel-prizewinning doctor.

Electroconvulsive therapy (ECT), or electric shock treatment, was once normal in mental hospitals, though there is no verifiabl sci-entific evidence that it benefits patients. A reason why the husband of

"Anna" – my friend's sister-in-law who burned herself to death – went along with the recommendation of R. D. Laing was his desperate and entirely understandable hope that therapy might enable his wife to break out of a vicious circle of repeated breakdowns and hospitalisations. When Anna was in the hospital, her doctors had demanded that she receive ECT, despite anguished objections from her husband. Laing's insistence on hearing the complaints of people who heard voices, suffered from hallucinations, and were filled with paranoid fears was well ahead of his time. Otherwise, his approach was intellectually self-indulgent, unscientific, and damaging to those he sought to help. Patients' families suffered appallingly because he blamed them for their children's insanity. Unfortunately, the failure of Laingian therapies to help patients discredited "talk therapy" as a whole and encouraged total reliance on medication as a treatment.

The wheel has now turned full circle since the 1970s, and today it is the purely biological explanations for schizophrenia that are being questioned as never before. These hypotheses about the cause and course of mental disorders have not been scientifically proved despite many tests and trials. Critics of the psychiatric establishment, particularly in Europe, allege that its diagnoses – even the distinction between schizophrenia and bipolar disorder – are artificial constructs and do not correspond to verifiable categories. Even so, these diseases have dominated psychiatry for a hundred years, ever since they were first described in the pioneering work of the German doctor and researcher Emil Kraepelin, born in 1856. Far more influential than Freud's ideas in establishing the intellectual framework by which psychosis was diagnosed and studied, Kraepelin's conception of mental illness now seems schematic in form but vague on specifics. Schizophrenia and bipolar disorder are often spoken of by laypeople – I used to do so myself – as if they were definitions as precise as those for hepatitis or appendicitis. In reality, the names are no more than those given to a collection of symptoms observable at a certain moment in time. A person is diagnosed as having some type of mental disorder depending on which items in a checklist of symptoms appear applicable to his or her condition. These diagnoses are very hazy compared to those in physical medicine, though the family of the person examined may think they are as precise as the diagnosis of a broken leg.

For example, paranoid schizophrenia is typified by exaggerated suspicions of others and fear of persecutory schemes. Disorganised or hebephrenic schizophrenia is signified by verbal incoherence and moods and emotions not appropriate to a situation. But the dividing wall between the two conditions is curiously permeable, as they often are between other categories of mental illness; they are in fact loose and all-embracing. Schizoaffective disorder, for instance, is a mix of symptoms of schizophrenia and a mood disorder such as a serious depression. "The conventional approach to understanding madness is deeply flawed," believes Richard P. Bentall, a professor of clinical psychology at the University of Bangor in Wales and a leading critic of the traditional approach. "This is why there has been so little progress in the treatment of psychiatric disorders since the time of Kraepelin. Most researchers and clinicians have been stuck at the end of the blind alley into which he led us a century ago."

Some of what I thought I was learning about schizophrenia under ten years ago is unravelling as tests become more rigorous and scientific. I had read with great interest in early 2002, when Henry was first ill, that the incidence of schizophrenia was 1 per cent of the population in all countries, according to a World Health Organization

(WHO) study. The figure remained the same whether you were in Nairobi or New York, Copenhagen or Jakarta, the third or developed world. I found this extraordinary, since I did not know of any other ailment which had such a uniform incidence. If true, the statistical uniformity must mean that differing environment plays no role in determining whether or not somebody would develop schizophrenia. If the children of Wall Street bankers and Australian aborigines are equally prone, then the propensity to suffer from the disorder is hardwired into everybody's genes. Given that the aborigines arrived in Australia tens of thousands of years ago, this hardwiring happened at an early stage in the history of the human race.

Like so many apparently hard facts about schizophrenia, the WHO figures turned out to be dubious. It appears that the incidence of the disorder differs not only between countries but also within countries and between people who live in cities, towns, and villages. Environmental factors demonstrably interact with a genetic predisposition to trigger different variants of a mental disorder that cannot have a solely biological origin. For instance, numerous surveys and tests all show that West Indian immigrants to Britain are six times more likely to get schizophrenia than whites long resident there. West Indians who remain living in the Caribbean have normal levels of the disorder. Other studies show that migrant communities in different parts of the world are likewise highly vulnerable to schizophrenia. Presumably, enhanced insecurity – familial, social, economic, and political – must play a role. Explaining why this should be so is made all the more difficult because diagnoses around the world employ almost comically different criteria. The highly authoritative manual of the American Psychiatric Association says that a diagnosis of schizophrenia should come only after six months' observation, while the WHO's criteria, used in Europe and much of the rest of the world, allows for a diagnosis after only one month. Not surprisingly, diagnosed Europeans are far more resilient than Americans in recovering from schizophrenia, as they have been suffering from it for a shorter period.

A further worrying sign that traditional diagnoses are highly arbitrary is that the same individual may receive radically different diagnoses at different times. Dr Robin Murray, one of the pioneers of new thinking about schizophrenia, says that it is not uncommon to see somebody who has been admitted to a hospital many times, and "maybe five times they had a diagnosis of schizophrenia, three times they had a diagnosis of schizo-affective disorder, and a couple of times they've had a diagnosis of bipolar disorder." He recalls exclaiming angrily about one case, "It's absolutely clear this is bipolar disorder. Who are the idiots who diagnosed schizophrenia in the past?" A grinning doctor pointed out that Dr Murray had made the original diagnosis himself. The problem with schizophrenia, he adds, is that "like pain or breathlessness, it's purely a symptomatic process."

A new picture of schizophrenia has begun to emerge over the last ten years, portraying it as having a series of causes rather than one single cause. There is undoubtedly a large genetic component. However, it appears that it is not the creation of a dominant gene but of a significant number of less powerful genes which interact with one another and with environmental factors. The genes do not cause schizophrenia but come into play when they are triggered by events. In other words, possession of these inherited genes does not doom a person to insanity, though it does make him or her vulnerable. Environmental factors that have been shown to play a role include obstetric problems; living in the city rather than the country; taking particular drugs such as cannabis, cocaine, or amphetamines; or being a newly arrived immigrant.

Nothing in schizophrenia is simple, and cause and effect can be interpreted in different ways. Poor people living in the centre of cities have a greater incidence of the disorder. This may be because the poor suffer the stresses of poverty, and in some this triggers schizophrenia; it could also mean that people who have it cannot work and become impoverished. There are other signs that accentuated social and psychological stresses trigger a psychotic crisis in young men, which may explain the high proportion of breakdowns during their first year away from home at school or university or doing military service. In the case of cannabis, three quarters of consumers may be able to take it with no ill effect, but the remaining quarter, the genetically vulnerable, play Russian roulette.

Research is starting to deepen our understanding of how brain chemistry, when altered and confused for whatever biological, social, or psychological reason, produces the symptoms which lead to breakdown. One of the most dramatic and interesting symptoms is "hearing voices," and these auditory hallucinations were central to Henry's psychosis. To him, his voices and visions were as real as conversations with me or his friends, while to doctors and nurses they were signs that he was still sick and should probably receive a higher dose of medication. Brain imaging shows how people with schizophrenia really do hear voices, but they are a misdirection of the "inner speech" we all create and listen to. Such speech is made up of verbalised but unexpressed thoughts, imaginary conversations and arguments, bits of dialogue which are never spoken. In the case of somebody suffering from schizophrenia, this inner speech is received through the part of the brain handling the reception of external speech, so it appears to come from a separate entity. No wonder that to Henry, the commands and comments of trees and bushes, as well as the voices of friends both alive and dead, sounded so real. When he saw a golden Buddha hovering over Brighton Beach, or climbed to reach the Hanging Gardens of Babylon on the other side of a railway viaduct, these were dreams made flesh, part of a magical world he found deeply attractive.

The distinction between schizophrenia and other mental disorders appears much less solid today than it did during most of the twentieth century. So, too, does the belief that there is a deep divide between madness and normality; the symptoms of the former are often evident at a lower intensity in people who see no reason ever to go near a psychiatrist or a mental hospital. The picture is different from that traditionally portrayed in the New Testament or in scenes in medieval glass, where the insane are possessed by devils until these are evicted through divine power. In reality, some 10 to 20 per cent of the population occupies an intermediate zone between normality and psychosis. As many as one in ten people hear voices not dissimilar from those Henry heard urging him on his barefoot journeys through the countryside. Others harbour irrational suspicions of their neighbours or colleagues, see themselves as victims of persecution, or have an exaggerated conviction that their phone is bugged and they are being followed by the CIA. This intermediate stage is variously called schizotypal, schizoid, schizophrenia spectrum, or schizotaxic and is difficult to investigate because people fear that if they are too forthcoming about voices or exotic fears and suspicions, they will be seen as mad.

Doctors are becoming less categorical about immediately prescribing medication for those admitting to hearing external voices. Some, such as Henry, need medication as swiftly as possible, and fullblown schizophrenia and psychosis do exist, but psychosis no longer appears as an island of insanity cut off by deep channels from the normal and the sane. People who develop schizophrenia have often previously shown schizoid tendencies, which, in some cases, become highly intensified and destructive. Many mental health practitioners Jan and I spoke to said there was no therapy for schizophrenia but medication and that this would not provide a total cure. But we wondered if there was a road back from full-blown schizophrenia to an intermediate zone where the gusts of irrationality were less strong and where something closer to a normal life could be lived.

One man who has made this difficult journey successfully is Mark Lawrence, who today runs a small pharmaceutical company in Oxford. An articulate and perceptive man, he told me of his experience of schizophrenia after reading an article about it by Henry and me. Mark said his experience was somewhat similar to Henry's, though he has since recovered from his psychosis with a minimum of clinical intervention. He was twenty-six years old when his hallucinations started, and he believes his symptoms were as florid as Henry's. Possibly his age, compared to Henry's twenty years at the onset of his disorder, made all the difference in Mark's ability to survive outside a hospital. "I was a dope-smoking artist squatting in Berlin," recalls Mark. "I was convinced that my visions were a spiritual awakening and not symptomatic of any illness." He believes that at the time he had every known symptom of schizophrenia. "Yet I want to emphasise to you," he adds, "that the spiritual reckoning – and the ascetic phase I went through – were important to my recovery. As Henry says of his condition, the state I was in produced the best time of my life. Compare it to a wild love affair, and you might begin to appreciate the sense of deep enchantment and motivation I felt." He recognises now that his mind was deeply disordered. "I was once convinced," he says, "that if I didn't walk to Bosham Harbour and perform a ritual by four P.M., the world was going to end."

Mark's road to recovery gives weight to the thesis that many aspects of schizophrenia are highly exaggerated forms of ordinary human behaviour. He says, "The key was finding the space to explore my mind without further distortion from prescription drugs or from concerned relatives. As it happens, this was not a mental hospital but a job as an evening steward in an army officers' mess, a job so quiet and undemanding that it was practically a sinecure. I spent evenings sitting in an armchair, reading, thinking, and very occasionally serving officers. Many psychiatrists would shy away from this approach, fearing that it feeds delusions, but I simply meditated and bided my time." Mark felt that his beliefs – though a psychiatrist might view them as irrational – were not so different from traditional religious or spiritual beliefs. His father, an atheist, was horrified by this notion and "saw my eccentric spiritual interests or pronouncements as totally delusional. But they weren't quite, at least not totally." Mark visited monasteries and found speaking to monks useful in establishing a balance between his spiritual feelings and the real world. "Like anybody settling down in any good relationship, the monks themselves are often veterans of implacable fervour that inevitably gives way to something less foolhardy. Quakers are a good source of support, too. You can hardly feel yourself to be an outsider when an entire meetinghouse of people is silently engaged in dwelling on the otherworldly and the inspirational."

Mark recovered from his psychoses, produced a dissertation on the physiology of hearing voices for his bachelor's of science, and went to Oxford to carry out clinical research in this area. He got married, set up his company, and says, "I generally enjoy my sanity." His meetings with monks and Quakers helped him put his own experiences in a more manageable context. "Meeting monks didn't make me want to become one, but they did make me realise that intense spiritual/artistic feelings need a counterbalance in ordinary life." It was important for him to be with people who took the idea of spiritual visions seriously as a path towards self-knowledge and did not see them in purely medical terms. This was never going to happen at any of the hospitals Henry was in. Mark remarks, "NHS psychiatrists and nurses are akin to foreign correspondents, in that the occupational hazard is being jaded and cynical." He says he is not anti-psychiatrist, but to see schizophrenia as a purely medical problem is too limited and itself becomes an obstacle to a return to normal life. A further benefit of seeing personal voices and visions in the context of generally accepted spiritual or religious life is that it makes these phenomena appear less outré, easing the way for somebody suffering from a mental disorder to escape the terrible fear that he has indeed gone mad. Mark's description of his visions and voices was very similar to Henry's. I wondered if Henry, too, would one day escape his psychosis. I also wondered if there had ever been a time when he could have got better without medication and being sent to a mental hospital. The difference between him and Mark was that when Henry did not take his medication and was not in the hospital, his condition rapidly grew worse. Even at his best, he could not have coped with light duties in an officers' mess because his mind was too chaotic. Jan and I were always frightened when he ran away, but we looked hopefully for signs that he could care for himself only to find that time and again he slid into dementia within a couple of days.

The picture I have today of schizophrenia is very different from the one I had soon after Henry was diagnosed. Its nature is far more elusive and difficult to define than I imagined. It is even possible for two people to be diagnosed as suffering from schizophrenia without having a single symptom in common. The same cannot be said of any physical ailment.

CHAPTER NINE
Patrick

One of the first questions Jan and I were asked by doctors when Henry was originally admitted to the hospital was whether there was any history of mental disorder in either of our families. That schizophrenia and bipolar disorder are in part hereditary remains one of the few hypotheses about mental illness that has stood the test of time. Studies show that the child of nonschizophrenic parents unlucky enough to be adopted into a family in which a parent is schizophrenic does not become more susceptible to the disease. However, a child with a schizophrenic parent who is adopted into a nonschizophrenic family has a higher than normal likelihood of getting schizophrenia.

Neither Jan nor I had ever been diagnosed with a mental disorder. Jan had suffered on occasion from severe depression brought on by her own ill health, a series of bereavements of close relatives, and overwork at her university, but these depressions never amounted to a psychosis. As I looked at our relatives past and present for signs of mental illness, it struck me that most of them were highly intelligent men and women who had done well in their professions, be they journalists, academics, clergy, or businessmen. Henry pointed out that his parents and grandparents had all written books. Our family backgrounds fit in with the belief that families susceptible to schizophrenia have a higher proportion than normal of exceptionally able, intelligent, and energetic people. The cases of James Joyce's daughter, Albert Einstein's son, and Carl Jung's mother are commonly cited as evidence. I had previously been dubious about this supposed connection between intelligence and originality with schizophrenia, as I suspected it might be a form of emotional compensation for families who discovered they were susceptible to the disease, but I couldn't dismiss it altogether. In any case, the process by which the disorder is transmitted is not simple; genetic vulnerability is a factor, though 63 per cent of people with the disorder have no identifiable family history of the disease. My initial doubts began to give way as I discovered the astonishing number of my friends, whom I thought of as highly intelligent who had close relatives suffering from schizophrenia.

As I began to follow the genetic gunpowder trail which might explain Henry's disorder, I tried not to see every mental ailment that had ever beset anybody in Jan's family or my own as a sinister signpost to what lay ahead for Henry. Being high-strung does not necessarily imply schizophrenic susceptibility. In the case of my own parents, Claud and Patricia Cockburn, there were no traces of any mental disorder; both were highly self-confident and tough-minded. A radical journalist and author, my father seldom showed the strain of very poor health and persistent financial crises. My mother was similarly strong-willed and resilient in the face of setbacks. She was self-educated to a high level and an excellent organiser. At the age of twenty-three, she led an expedition on behalf of the Royal Geographical Society through the forests of Central Africa to make a map of languages spoken in the Congo.

Jan's parents, Hugh and Elisabeth Montefiore, came from very different backgrounds, his being wealthy and Jewish and hers being hard up but highly educated Christians. After a spectacular and unexpected conversion to Christianity as a schoolboy, Hugh became bishop of Birmingham, a member of the House of Lords, and a leader of the Anglican Church. This was all the more surprising since he was not only Jewish but was born into a family, the Sebag-Montefiores, who were highly conscious of being members of the so-called Cousinhood, the interrelated Anglo-Jewish financial aristocracy who had flourished in the City of London since the seventeenth century. The circumstances of Hugh's conversion made me think of Henry because he, too, believed he had seen a vision and heard a voice, the reality of which he wholly believed in and which was to change his entire life. His experience highlighted for me that it was possible to have some of the symptoms of schizophrenia without being mad or being seen as suffering from madness. The history of religion revolves around men and women, like the prophet Mohammed or Joan of Arc, who believed they directly received divine instruction through visions and voices. I wondered if there might be a common genetic explanation for what had happened to Hugh and to Henry.

When Hugh was a sixteen-year-old schoolboy at Rugby School in England in the winter of 1936, he believed Jesus appeared to him and told him to become a Christian. He wrote a detailed account: "I suddenly became aware of a figure in white whom I saw clearly in my mind's eye. I heard the words 'Follow me.' Instinctively, I knew that this was Jesus, heaven knows how. I knew nothing about him. Put like that, it sounds somewhat bare; in fact, it was an indescribably rich event that filled me afterwards with overpowering joy. I could do no other than to follow those instructions . . . I was aware of the living Christ, and because of that, I was aware of God in a new way." Other than Hugh's unshakable conviction that he had received a divine order, there had been no preliminary signs leading up to his conversion. He had never attended a Christian service, had thought of becoming a rabbi, was not dissatisfied with Judaism, and nobody had tried to proselytise him. He found it difficult to describe what had happened: "Any verbal description sounds rather bare and banal. Deep religious experience is always indescribable and usually incommunicable."

Determined to be baptised, Hugh was appalled by the necessity of announcing it to his parents, Charles and Muriel Sebag-Montefiore, both of whom were devout and practicing Jews. He was well aware that his sudden conversion to Christianity would be seen as inexplicable and scandalous by most people he had grown up with. "It is difficult to explain to Gentiles how Jews feel about this," he said, reflecting on Jewish reaction to his conversion. "It was like treason; it was a spiritual betrayal, as Jews see it, of all that earlier Jews had lived and died for." Baptism of a Jew evoked folk memories of forced conversions to escape persecution or voluntary ones in pursuit of wealth and power. An ancestor of his mother's family, the de Passes, was burned to death by the Spanish Inquisition and was heard reciting the Shema, the Jewish equivalent of the Lord's Prayer, as the flames rose around him. Hugh's relatives were particularly conscious of being Jewish because of their descent from the great Jewish philanthropist and patriarch Sir Moses Montefiore, who had devoted his long life – he lived to be a hundred – to charitable work and stopping pogroms of Jews in Eastern Europe and the Middle East. The implications of what happened to Hugh did not escape the authorities of his school, who were terrified of scandal, if they were accused of having a hand in his conversion. When Hugh asked to be baptised, his headmaster at Rugby curtly dismissed the whole idea.

"But sir – Jesus told me to do this," said Hugh, presumably hoping that divine sponsorship would make his decision more acceptable.

"I don't care who told you, Sebag-Montefiore," replied his headmaster. "You belong to an extremely eminent Jewish family, and I do not wish to stir up a hornet's nest."

When Hugh did tell his parents, they behaved with great restraint and asked him to wait a year before being baptised but otherwise did not attempt to change his mind. He himself felt, if anything, more Jewish following his conversion, saying, "After all, Jesus was a Jew, and I could only understand Christianity as the fulfilment of Judaism." Nevertheless, he said later that he never felt wholly accepted by the Anglican Church, even when he was among its leaders. He was an able and highly energetic man, restlessly throwing out new ideas like small firecrackers. I thought it a pity that he spent his entire career in three organisations – the Anglican Church, the upper ranks of academia at Cambridge University, and the British army during World War II – that even by British standards were notoriously slow-moving and sclerotic. So far as I know, he never saw another vision, but his descriptions of what he saw and heard were very similar to what Henry told me of his experiences.

There was further evidence that Hugh's family had a genetic predisposition to schizotypy, which might produce originality of thought but might also lead to a mental disorder, and this susceptibility had been inherited by Henry. Going back one more generation, Hugh's mother, Muriel de Pass, had been confined in a mental hospital several times. At first her extended family thought she suffered from hypochondria. Mysterious lumps appeared on her body, and she liked to go to quack nursing homes for cures, once living on orange juice for twenty-eight days. Her problems were exacerbated by a simple lack of anything to do. She and her husband, Charles, were born rich, and he, a highly successful stockbroker, became even wealthier. Eight servants, not including the chauffeur and nanny, looked after them in a vast mansion overlooking Kensington Gardens in central London, which later became the Israeli embassy. Hugh believed that the only time his mother was truly happy was when she was swabbing floors for the Women's Voluntary Service during the war. Afterwards her mood swings between elation and depression grew worse, and she was diagnosed with what was then called manic depression (now bipolar disorder). Sectioned for short periods, Hugh says, she was "put in a home where she was forced to have electric shock treatment which she very properly hated and feared."

Hugh's wife, Elisabeth, a highly intelligent woman though at times a victim of depression, came from a vigorously intellectual family. She was one of six children of a Presbyterian missionary who founded the World Council of Churches; all of the children went to Oxford on scholarships and money borrowed from the bank. The only exception, denied a place at Oxford because the family money had run out entirely, worked during the war breaking German codes. By a strange coincidence, one of Elisabeth's brothers was Sir William Paton, professor of pharmacology at Oxford, whose research was very relevant to what was to happen to Henry. One of the world's greatest experts on cannabis, Sir William published many papers with his colleagues in the 1970s, revealing for the first time evidence that even limited social use of cannabis could precipitate schizophrenia in people who previously had no psychological problems. He discovered that even smoking a single joint at a Christmas party could induce schizophrenia-like symptoms such as hallucinations, paranoia, fragmented thought processes, mood swings between laughing and crying, and tedious repetition of the same thought. These were not fashionable ideas in Oxford in the 1970s, when students had just started taking cannabis on a mass scale, but Sir William's findings were confirmed by a series of other studies. A US study found that after cannabis became widely available in the US Army in Europe, the incidence of schizophrenia among army personnel increased thirty-eight-fold from 1967 to 1971.

Henry was never very interested in my research into the mental health of his ancestors. This was hardly surprising, since he did not admit to being ill; he certainly did not want to think about the question of inherited vulnerability to schizophrenia. But Sir Moses Montefiore and his wealthy Jewish ancestors did enter our lives in an unexpected and peculiar way.

After Henry moved to the halfway house called the Grove – located in the run-down holiday resort and small port of Ramsgate on the Isle of Thanet, overlooking the Channel, some fifteen miles from Canterbury – I would visit him there, and we would sit on the beach or walk out along the pier that enclosed the harbour. I knew that since his breakdown, Henry liked to walk in woods as wild and remote as possible. I recalled that Sir Moses, after making a large fortune and retiring from business at the age of forty to devote his life to good works, had owned a large house and estate called East Cliff Lodge in Ramsgate, which was popular with the aristocracy in the early nineteenth century. He had reputedly given a golden key to the extensive grounds to Queen Victoria, who lived in a nearby villa in Ramsgate before she was crowned. The little town later fell into decay and become moribund as trains and planes enabled people from London to travel rapidly to warmer resorts on the continent. Its grand houses were abandoned or divided up, to be occupied by pensioners in need of cheap accommodation. East Cliff Lodge was pulled down, only the substantial greenhouse surviving, and its neat gardens turned into a jungle of overgrown bushes and tall trees. Jan, Henry, and I used to walk about there and sometimes bring a picnic. We stumbled upon a well-maintained though seldom visited synagogue half hidden in a grove of trees and, close by, a monument to Sir Moses. The abandoned estate and the occasional signs of past magnificence exuded a sense of gloom, but the place also had for us the allure of a secret garden. My mood may have been affected by worry about Henry, but I found these dilapidated remains less depressing than the rest of Ramsgate.

I looked back at my own family's history, searching for signs of mental disorder or distress. My ancestors came from different parts of England, Scotland, and Ireland: on my mother's side, they were a mixture of Anglo-Irish landowners and policemen and English bankers and army officers. They were often eccentric, but I could find nothing that hinted at a hereditary mental disorder. My grandfather on my father's side of the family was named Henry Cockburn and had spent thirty years as a British diplomat in China before becoming the British minister in Korea. He resigned from the Foreign Office after being forced to hand over a dissident Korean journalist, whom he was convinced would be tortured, to the Japanese authorities occupying the country.

The most interesting fact I knew about my great-grandfather Francis Jeffrey Cockburn, who became a judge in India, was that as a boy in Edinburgh, he had blown off his right hand when playing with a flask of gunpowder near an open fire. His family kept the remains of his amputated hand in a glass of spirits on the mantelpiece and would show it to visitors as an interesting curio. His father, after whom my son was named, was Lord Henry Cockburn, a judge, reformer, and writer famous in Scotland. None of these forebears was known to have suffered from any mental disorder, though I knew more about the men than the women, and I wondered how many of them, like Muriel de Pass, had suffered from an ailment that had been dismissed at the time as hypochondria.

There was one exception to this apparently unrelenting record of total sanity: Evelyn Waugh, one of the great English novelists of the twentieth century and a great-grandson of Lord Cockburn, which made him a distant cousin of Henry and me. He not only suffered a spectacular bout of what he called madness but also wrote an extraordinarily vivid account of it in his short novel *The Ordeal of Gilbert Pinfold*, which he freely admitted was a thinly disguised account of what had happened to him on a 1954 voyage to Ceylon to restore his health.

He described how he was pursued by voices and paranoid terrors that appeared wholly real. Even when he recovered and the voices had fallen silent, his recollection of them retained its vividness. "No sound troubled him from that other half-world into which he had stumbled but there was nothing dreamlike about his memories," wrote Waugh. "They remained undiminished and unobscured, as sharp and hard as any event of his waking life."

Waugh always referred to himself as being mad for a time. Typically, his friends were eager to avoid calling his breakdown even temporary insanity and blamed it on the large amounts of bromide and chloral he was taking for sleep, on top of his usual heavy consumption of brandy, wine, and crème de menthe. This certainly was an immediate cause, but the identifiable physical cause does not mean he was not quite mad for a period of time. Nor does it explain why he but not others should react to too many drugs and too much alcohol by becoming temporarily insane. He believed he might have been possessed by devils, and on his return to London, his first act was to ask a priest to exorcise him.

Waugh's account of Pinfold's "madness" is compelling. Pinfold, a middle-aged writer living in the country, goes abroad because he is already in poor health, but from the moment he enters his cabin on a ship called the *Caliban*, bound for Ceylon, he hears voices denigrating him. He becomes convinced that the pipes and electric wiring in the ceiling of his cabin are a gigantic broadcasting mechanism, a relic of the vessel's wartime service somehow enabling him to hear other passengers conspiring against him, as well as a jazz orchestra that never stops playing. Pinfold listens to the ship's captain and a woman he nicknames "Goneril" torture to death a member of the crew. Some of this persecution is petty. He waits, stick in hand, to confront two thuggish young men he has overheard planning to break into his cabin in the middle of the night and assault him. He gives telegrams to the ship's radio officer, who reads them out to other passengers, who roar with laughter. Pinfold becomes convinced that the *Caliban* is going to be boarded and detained by a Spanish vessel as part of an international crisis between Spain and Britain over possession of Gibraltar. In the midst of this, Pinfold suspects he is going insane, and when he discovers he is being hoaxed by enemies among the passengers, he is relieved: "He might be unpopular; he might be ridiculous; but he was not mad."

Waugh's actual experiences differed from Pinfold's in two significant respects. Friends had observed something was wrong with him before he left on his voyage. He was suffering from a growing persecution mania, much of it to do with BBC interviewers, and, while previously querulous, he had become much more aggressive and rude. The second difference was that Waugh was much more reluctant to admit that he was suffering from delusions. The whole affair sounds like a nightmare for Waugh and his fictional counterpart, but surprisingly, as with Henry, his horrible voyage had its attractive side. "But it *was* exciting," says Pinfold to his wife as they drive home. "It was the most exciting thing, really, that ever happened to me."

Waugh was probably too distant a relative from whom Henry could have inherited a susceptibility towards psychosis. But the experiences of Evelyn Waugh and Hugh Montefiore, who had little in common other than being very religious, tend to confirm recent hypotheses about schizophrenia. First, the genetic inheritance that produces schizophrenia or bipolar disorder is related to the genetic combination endowing people with exceptionally original and creative minds. Second, Hugh's voices and Waugh's delusions show that some symptoms of schizophrenia can occur in those otherwise regarded as sane, and do not mean they are mad. What Henry believed he heard and saw was not so different from the experiences of his grandfather and his cousin except that in his case, the voices never stopped. And like Waugh, he was highly excited by the dreamworld of his psychosis.

Chapter Ten

Henry

I was moved from Anselm after about six months to a rehabilitation cen- tre in Ramsgate called the Grove. It was near the sea, and I would walk the whole length of the seafront, from Ramsgate to Broadstairs. Near the house I discovered a giant plum tree, and I would drag my dad there to eat fresh plums. I felt I wanted to have once again the experiences of the pre- vious autumn – talking to trees and following the wind. Most of the time, I was spitting out my medication. I wanted to run away because running away had become crucial to my life. I felt for a moment that I was being liberated and I was being brave. My plan was to walk to Canterbury, about fifteen miles away, and I went by the railway line after walking through a few fields. I remember walking through a cornfield where there was a huge spiderweb. I jumped over it, and the spider looked crossly at me as if I should have walked through his web. I went by the railway line and took my shoes off. The tree talked to me in a sort of Shakespearian rhyme:

> *You must not act the knave*
> *When others rant and rave.*

I asked about the monsoon that the tree I had talked to nearly two years earlier had predicted, and it said, "The towers will be surrounded by water" (I thought the tree meant the enormous towers of the power station near Ramsgate). I walked on a little and heard a very loud woof, and a big dog was staring at me. I took my clothes off and felt cold. I walked by the train tracks until I stepped on a thorn and fell over just seconds before a train raced past. I was lucky that I wasn't seen. If someone had seen a naked man walking by the train tracks, they would have told the police. I could see the two towers near Ramsgate, and I knew it would be a long way to Canterbury. At first I walked through the bracken that grows by the railway tracks. Then I decided to walk by a field that was covered in thistles. This hurt my feet. I got to a ditch that had water in it. I rested there until dawn and it was very cold. When the day broke, it was misty and I ran round the side of a farm, though I was completely naked. I was hoping to get to a motorway where the police might pick me up. I followed a ditch and eventually it led me to the motorway. I heard a duck quack and it went into a tunnel under the motorway. I walked past some hawthorn trees, through a car park, over a fence, and there was the River Stour.

I swam across the river and walked across a field towards the sea. I felt I was a nomad walking the plains. In the distance I could see people mushroom-picking. When I got to the sea, there was a man who was also naked and was smoking a cigarette. I thought I was in the right place and there were others like me who were following the winds and going naked. I kept walking along the coast, but there were no more naked people. I saw a woman who looked at me with contempt and said, "You can't come down here. The nudist beach is back that way."

I had cut myself on some barbed wire and there were flies everywhere, but I walked back to the river and swam it again. I got into a boat on the other side and found a pair of overalls. I went through an industrial estate and a man told me I was on private property. My feet were killing me, and the stony gravel made them all the more painful. I wrapped pieces of a plastic bag around them, but even with these makeshift shoes, my feet were still sore. I walked along the river, the wind urging me forward, until I got to Sandwich. I scrounged an apple and my feet were hurting so much that I tried hitchhiking. A friendly man and his daughter stopped and asked me where I wanted to go. I said, "Canterbury or Ramsgate." They said they were going to Ramsgate, so I hopped in. My journey, which had taken a day on foot, took about ten minutes by car. I went back to the Grove, where the doctor suggested I take a new drug called clozapine. I ran away several more times from Ramsgate. Once I felt the trees urging me to take my clothes off and some kids saw me and said, "Look at the caveman." Twice I was picked up by the police, and finally they sent me back to Anselm ward in Canterbury.

After a couple of weeks they began to let me go out again. I ate roasted sunflower seeds, leaving a path of shells wherever I walked. I spent most of my time in Greyfriars Gardens with teenagers who were smoking dope and playing cards. I wasn't smoking dope at the time, but I joined in when they were playing cards. From Anselm, I was transferred first to Amber ward and then to a halfway house on Ethelbert Road. Everybody there had to take a turn cooking, and we kept the house spotless. I had one friend there, a white Rasta with orange dreadlocks. He had a pair of turntables in his room, and I would sit there while he DJ'ed. I went on long walks and was desperate to get away. I was spitting out my medication. When it came time for me to have a blood test (you have to have a blood test for clozapine because it can affect your white blood cells), I took an overdose so they wouldn't know I hadn't been taking it. Unfortunately, it didn't enter my bloodstream quick enough, so they found out anyway. I was sectioned again, and once again I ran away.

It started to snow. I sat under a tree for two days. I was quite dehydrated, so I ate bits of snow that fell from the tree that I was under. I sat there wondering about my life. When I was closest to death, I thought I saw a vision of my friend Luke and then a vision of Elisa, the girl I was in love with. I sat there in the tree surrounded by snow. Occasionally, I would take a dip in the freezing-cold river. After two days I decided to move. My feet were completely numb. I walked through the snow naked. A man appeared and said, "What are you doing?" He took me into his house, and a lady there wrapped a towel around me. I asked for some orange juice and she gave me some. She sat there rubbing my feet to get them warm. Unfortunately, she did it too fast because I got frostbite. An ambulance came to pick me up. I sat there singing rap poetry as they hauled me into the ambulance. When I got to the hospital, my mother and her friend Nicky were there. The doctor wanted to cut my toes off, but I wouldn't consent to this. They did look blue at first, but they regained their colour. My feet were in a lot of pain because they had been warmed up too quickly. The doctor from the halfway house, a Dr Vile, came to tell me he had sectioned me again. The nights in the general hospital were uncomfortable and my feet were really hurting. I shouted for painkillers, but nobody came at first.

I was moved back to Anselm, but it was easy to get out of. Once I climbed up a drainpipe and along a gutter to avoid a fence around the ward and escaped into the bushes. I could see people looking for me in the faint light of dusk. I stripped and made my way over the golf course and crossed the road when it was clear. I walked into the undergrowth at about midnight. All the bushes seemed to point their branches towards me, and I touched the buds. In my mind's eye, I could see a black cat and an owl looking at me. I feared they would betray my whereabouts to people, for I could see their yellow eyes. As I stood there naked in the wood, I saw a giant worm come down from the heavens. It made a giant loop and went back up to the heavens. I put my finger in the loop and could feel the scales against my hand. If I had moved my finger too fast, it would have cut my hand, as the scales were sharp.

I sat under a tree and the tree started to move. Its root touched my finger as I held my breath. It was like being next to the train tracks in Brighton all those months ago. It told me to come to London. I sat under the tree until the morning, touching the root. Then a robin landed near my shoulder and darted away again. I tried to find my way by holding my breath until I lost control of my movements. I got into a swamp near the golf course very slowly because it was ice-cold. I could see little mushrooms growing in front of me. I felt like the place was telling me to go to a thornbush, so I went and sat under it. It said what the tree had said earlier – that I should go to London. It said I should go to Hackney, where they "don't go to school half the time, because all they do is rhyme."

I knew I was going to DVH – Dudley Venables House – the low-secure unit at St Martin's, before I actually went there. "Low-secure" does not fully describe what it is like. "High-secure" means Broadmoor – a prison for the criminally insane. "Medium-secure" is a step down from that. "Low-secure" makes it sound as if it is easy to get out of, but in fact there were two locked doors to get through, and the small open-air yard had a twelve-foot fence.

When I first went into DVH, I saw a woman who was heavily tattooed. I introduced myself as H instead of Henry. Near the door there was a man sitting next to two large plants; he had an electronic chessboard and was trying to beat the computer at chess. I had associated DVH with violence because when I was in the other wards and someone misbehaved, they would threaten him with being sent to DVH. Actually, it wasn't so bad, though before I came to the ward, two people had committed suicide in their bedrooms, so we were locked out of these from nine A.M. to ten P.M. I knew from Anselm ward the woman, Alison, who had hanged herself: she had a child, and she once made a beautiful pot in the pottery class. I remember doing a picture, and she complimented me, saying, "You could sell that for fifty pounds."

The ward had a nice smell to it. I greeted everyone there, and they were friendly. The smoking room was the main social place because most patients lived for their cigarettes. One man crushed metal ashtrays with his bare hands, and I was nervous of him at first because he said he did not like skinny types like me. At one time we – the patients in DVH – pretended that we were on a sailboat. Needless to say, I was the cabin boy. "I can smell rocks. Better keep away from these shores," said John, a Scottish guy from Aberdeen. I liked the staff. For the first week I didn't sleep at all. I lay under my Peruvian blanket on the floor, as I wasn't using a bed at that point.

Early on at DVH, there was a Rastafarian who had been put in the seclusion room, which is basically a cell where they put patients who were violent. Alison had cut her name into the wall. The Rasta, who was called Charlie, had been put there for head-butting the doctor. Charlie was in there for two weeks with nothing to read but the Bible and came out something of a religious fanatic. I saw him through the glass panes, and he pointed at me and said, "You're Jesus." Then he pointed to himself and said, "I'm John the Baptist." Then he tried to baptise me and threw water all over the window.

The day Charlie got out of the seclusion room, my friend Peter and his girlfriend, Françoise, a Madagascan girl living in France, came to see me. Charlie sprinkled a little bit of water on my neck and asked to borrow a cross off a big broad-shouldered man named

Roy. He said he was having troubles with the spirits, but he gave us the cross anyway. Then Charlie christened me with the cross, saying, "In the name of the Father, the Son, and the Holy Spirit." I felt closer to my brothers and sisters at DVH at that point. That night Charlie played the guitar, and so did Peter, and I sang rap songs. Everyone was listening and it was a good night. Later, after Peter and Françoise had left, one of the staff asked me for a urine sample. I realised he thought that anybody having a good time in a place like DVH must have been smoking marijuana.

It was not so surprising that he thought we were taking dope, because it was easy to get a lot of the time in DVH. Dope was the cause of one of the few fights I was involved in there. A guy named Simon said he would get me some dope, but he wanted the money first. He said he had someone waiting outside the ward with it, but I never saw the dope and never got my money back. One day I was listening to some dance music and decided I wasn't going to put up with this anymore. Just as I was thinking this, Simon appeared out of nowhere and punched me. I ran away down a corridor. Then I turned round and chased after him. It took eight staff to hold me back. Later that day the police were called and spoke to me, though naturally, I didn't tell them about the dope. I think Simon went back to prison — he had previously been in Broadmoor.

Small things led to fights. Once in the smoking room, I flicked a potato chip at a man who said he had a titanium skull because he had fallen off his motorcycle and smashed his head. I did not do it for any particular reason, but he punched me in the face and twisted my arm behind me until I was rescued by one of the staff.

I was always fascinated by the underworld, secret tunnels under the earth where people live. Once I thought I had found one in Brighton, full of people whom I could see only because the tips of their cigarettes glowed in the dark. I was convinced there was a secret door in DVH where patients and staff would go to smoke crack. I never found that trapdoor, though I suspected it might be under a lamp in a chill-out room that had lots of cushions and coloured lights.

I was full of fears. When I first went to DVH, I thought I was being bugged electronically, as did many other patients – though I can't see why anyone should want to bug a mental hospital. Everybody could hear a sort of bleeping coming from the smoke alarms. We would turn up the radio so they could not hear their signal. Under my Peruvian rug, I would have waking dreams. Once I had a dream that my dad had phoned me up. In the dream he said that God had told him not to go to dangerous places anymore.

A mental hospital is not a prison or even a police cell, but at night, when you look at the wall, they seem the same. You want to feel the night air against your lips and the streets beneath your feet. You want to run away, but you can't really escape, so you grit your teeth and consume a lot of tobacco and coffee and try to find your fellow patients interesting. But the tobacco only lasts so long, and you can drink only so much coffee. I had given up smoking cigarettes for a year and a half when I came to DVH, but once we were all in the smoking room, I thought the glowing tips of the cigarettes looked like holy fires. Soon I was smoking forty cigarettes a day. When you are locked up, life passes so slowly that you start thinking in numbers: how many minutes there are in a day, how many hours in a week, what would make a million hours. You start to look at the tiles on the floor and to guess how many there are. Everything in life is boring.

I was in DVH for two years, and I ran away seventeen times. Usually, I did it by climbing over the fence. Later, the medication made me put on weight, but in those days I was light and quick. The courtyard was only twenty square yards, but there was a drainpipe where the fence met the wall. I would use this to jump to the fence and run away. Other times I would wait for hours by the double doors at the entrance for somebody to leave them both open for a second at the same time. Then I would rush through. Still other times I would wait by the seclusion room in case somebody left a bunch of keys in the lock which would let me unlock the outside doors. Sometimes the nurses would take me for walks and I would run away then. It was never easy. I was about 20 per cent successful in my attempts to run away, and about 80 per cent of the time they would catch me. Harrowing though it was being locked up, my main reason for escaping was that the trees were calling me and I had to do it.

CHAPTER ELEVEN
Patrick and Jan

I was terrified every time Henry ran away. Jan and I came to dread the ringing of the phone at unlikely times because it might be the hospital or the police saying he had disappeared again. When he did so, I would doze on the sofa by the door late into the night, hoping I would hear his footfalls in the street. I thought there was a better than even chance he would die as he roamed the Kent countryside, instinctively drawn to lakes and rivers and near-freezing water. If Henry was not trying to commit suicide, he at least seemed powerfully drawn to suicidal actions. The only hopeful sign was that on occasions he showed an almost equally strong urge to preserve his own life. Once he even called an ambulance to help him after he swam in a freezing lake. But often his psychosis was so intense that I feared he could not calculate how close he was to death because his illness reduced his ability to feel pain or even know if his body was too hot or too cold. I thought it all too likely that one day, whether it happened on purpose or by accident, we would get a regretful call from the police saying it was all over.

It is almost impossible in retrospect to convey the sense of dread and imminent disaster that Jan and I felt hovering over us. Each time we heard that Henry had survived, these fearful emotions would evaporate only to recur when there was a new crisis. But once the all-pervasive anxiety had dissipated, it was impossible even moments later to recall fully what it had felt like. The only way to give a true sense is to reproduce what we wrote contemporaneously when we did not know if Henry was going to turn up alive or dead. During one particularly fraught fortnight starting in January 2004, Jan kept a detailed daily diary that gives the flavour of the emotional pummelling we endured. This was the period described by Henry when he sat in the snow for two days and got frostbite. From Jan's and my perspectives, this episode was more complicated, and considerably more dangerous, than in his account. Henry never showed any regret or remorse for the misery he inflicted on us through his disappearances over about five years. He remained affectionate with us and often sensitive to others, but he acted like what he did was taking place in a different world.

It would have been very difficult for a single parent to have endured these successive crises without collapsing under the strain. As Jan explains, even dealing with Henry for part of the week on a day-to-day basis was a stressful experience. A single person ultimately would have been ground down. While Jan and I could not have coped with Henry's psychosis separately, it had brought us together more firmly than ever. We also had the advantage of being relatively well off and had the strong support of our own families. We did not think we could cure Henry, but we did believe that we could sustain and strengthen the sane part of him – and there always was a sane Henry as well as a mad one – so that he would survive. For all the endless setbacks and disappointments, he did not die, and this was our main achievement during the years when he was locked up in mental hospitals.

The successive crises described here by Jan hit us by surprise just when Henry appeared to be getting better. Now aged twenty-two, he had been sectioned for over a year, during which he started off at St Martin's in Canterbury, then moved to the halfway house in Ramsgate, from which he absconded three times. He then returned to Anselm ward at St Martin's, where he was supposedly taking a newly prescribed anti-psychotic called clozapine, which seemed to have a positive impact. Henry once again socialised with people, watched TV, read the papers, and even read a book, *The Hobbit*, before Christmas 2003. He was moved to the Amber ward where the doctors judged that he was ready for rehabilitation, which meant he moved to the house on Ethelbert Road in Canterbury, where the staff would help him make the transition from living in a hospital to ordinary life. Henry was not particularly enthusiastic about this shift, since at Amber, he was required only to swallow his medication, go swimming, and do art therapy. He could go out when he wanted and take long walks around Canterbury.

Jan's diary starts with a telephone call in January 23 from me in Iraq, where I was reporting that month. Jan told me the latest news about Henry, which was mostly good. He was coming to the end of his Section 3, under which he was legally confined, and which had to be renewed every six months. The doctors had asked Jan if they should let this lapse so Henry would become an "informal" patient, but neither Jan nor I was confident that he was well enough. He had been coming home on weekends, as well as Tuesday and Thursday evenings, when he mostly watched television and played computer games with Alex. Jan told me she was feeling overburdened by cooking for both boys and simultaneously trying to do her own work, involving a heavy teaching load and writing a new lecture on *Lady Chatterley's Lover*. She complained that Henry seldom washed up or helped around the house. We agreed that she would go for a walk with him the following day, January 24, and talk to him about doing more to help as well as about his move to the Ethelbert Road halfway house. The next day was bright and sparkling after a week of murky drizzle. Jan made lunch before taking Henry for the walk. She describes what happened next in her diary:

I fixed a quick pasta and tomato sauce for us all (Henry being a vegan since he got ill, plus he won't eat potatoes or rice or grapes in any form, fresh or dried, which is a challenge to a cook's ingenuity). Henry seemed in a bad mood – he was sitting on the sofa looking darkly at nothing in particular. But he responded to the idea of a walk in the water meadows – a favourite walk of his, though he made a face when I put my gumboots on before starting. As usual he was wearing an old shirt, grubby trousers and grubby trainers – he refuses to wear underpants, socks, pullover or jacket. (We've been told this is an indirect result of schizophrenia upsetting the body's thermostat – he doesn't feel cold though he is cold.) But it's mild today anyway.

Once we get to the meadows, he cheers up – it's a lovely afternoon. The water meadows are sopping, I'm glad of my gumboots. Henry takes off his trainers to walk barefoot through the wet grass.

We reach the old embankment and look at the river, which is very full, the colour of weak milky coffee with too much water, full of swirling eddies and dimples. I observe that it looks a bit dangerous. Henry says no, you could swim in it. I say I don't think it'd be safe. He shrugs.

We walk up the old railway embankment under the thorn trees, both of us slipping a bit in the mud. We talk about his illness. He says wryly that being an art student seems likely to leave you in a mental hospital – several other people he knows there are ex-art students, or else musicians. We also talk about drugs – a friend of his (not a mental patient) has come off heroin, he gave it up while staying at a friend's farm and has stuck to it for three weeks now, though he still smokes cannabis. Henry doesn't now do any drugs, except presumably his prescribed anti-psychotics, nor tobacco nor alcohol nor tea nor coffee. I talk with H about his cannabis-smoking in the past. He says he did it a lot, far more than I knew: "Since I was fourteen I don't think I passed a period of more than two or three weeks without a spliff. [Corrects himself] No, once I was off for six weeks." I ask him how much did he smoke – more than one joint a day? He grins. "A lot more than that." And tells me it was about five. "But that had nothing to do with what got me into the hospital." I: "Why not?" H: "Because it was *after* I gave it all up that all this started." I say cautiously, "Perhaps it triggered something?" He disagrees, but at least he doesn't get angry. He says with pride that he hasn't had a drink (alcoholic) for at least eighteen months, and hasn't smoked for five. I am fairly pleased with this conversation; at least we've talked overtly about his illness, something we rarely do these days.

Later, I fix supper and afterwards demand that this time both brothers should wash up. They first resist, then argue about whose turn it is to wash and whose to dry. In the end Henry washes, very slowly, and Alex dries. But I'm not allowed to take myself off; H demands that I ask him and Alex a lot of riddles while they work. I recall – as I expect Henry is doing – the time when he was nine and made me ask him riddles all the way from Victoria Station to Canterbury, while small Alex dozed in his buggy – my recall of *The Oxford Book of Nursery Rhymes* and H's cogitations and answers just lasting the hour and a half which the train journey took.

I don't really like doing these riddles now – it feels like pretending things are as they were when the boys were children. They're young men now and shouldn't make this fuss about taking their turn with the dishes. (Of course the rehab place, unlike the hospital, makes H do this routinely, and he tries, often successfully, to skive at home.) And I shouldn't have to entertain them while they're doing it – H is virtually making that a condition. But I can't see what else I can do, short of causing a row. H goes at nine-thirty – the rehab place, unlike the hospital, insists he's punctually back by ten for his night medication. It's a bit of a relief when he does.

SUNDAY JAN 25. I spend the morning at the office, writing my lecture. Back home about two to find H there, again looking grim. I make chickpea and leek soup and preempt him sloping off by demanding that Henry wash up. Henry furious, saying he did it yesterday and it's Alex's turn. I feel thoroughly pissed off at all this fuss and say please will he do it. He shouts at me that it's not fair, I'm favouring Alex over him, I always take anyone else's side against him. (I guess he's thinking of the doctors?) He does it, with bad grace, and we leave it to drain. He goes off to play a DVD game, looking like a thundercloud.

At four P.M., it's clear and still light. I decide to walk in Blean Wood; would quite like to go by myself but feel I should offer H the chance to come, too. As on Saturday, he's sitting on the sofa looking darkly at nothing – more darkly than before. This time the prospect of a walk doesn't seem to cheer him, but he says he'll come, even though it means a (short) drive, which he doesn't like. He looks grimly at my gumboots but says nothing.

When we get to the wood, he's not at all conversational. He won't walk with me, he keeps dropping behind, thirty yards or more. When I stop for him to catch up, he won't speak to me or respond to my overtures. When I look back at his angry face with its long uncombed hair and beard, I think of a lion. I also remember, sadly, walking here with a much younger H, his warm little hand in mine, chattering away. Not anymore. He won't talk, and I think he's angry at walking on a well-trodden track (all the trails in Blean Wood are that by the end of a fine weekend). Or else still angry about the washing up? But that seems too trivial. I ask him, is something bothering him? But he just shakes his head.

He goes at nine-thirty and I am candidly relieved that I won't have to see him till Tuesday. Frankly, I feel like kicking him. I think, *He can visit, yes, but while I have any say in the matter, I will* not *share my whole life with somebody who regards being asked to take his turn at washing up as a personal insult.*

Jan gave her lecture on Monday and went to see her therapist in the nearby town of Faversham whose advice about Henry had proved wise in the past. She described the row about washing up and how impossible Henry was to live with all the time. The therapist said, "He's too ill to live with at the moment." Jan thought this was putting it too strongly.

MONDAY JAN 26. Teaching and admin keep me at it till six, then I come home and start supper. Feel I've earned a hot bath and have one while it's in the oven. Then the phone rings. It's Michelle, the manager of the rehab place [on Ethelbert Road], asking me casually if Henry's at home. I say no, why should he be? It's not Tuesday. She says, "Well, he's not in for tea, he went out at midday and he's not returned." In other words, he's disappeared. And the forecast is for snow.

Michelle goes on to tell me of a major scene last Friday of which I knew nothing. Henry, while on Clozaril, has to have a weekly blood test to check his white blood cell count. The rehab doctor had ordered another to test the level of Clozaril in his plasma. (This isn't routinely done, though it should have been.) The test showed a nil level, and H admitted to them that he hadn't been taking his pills for a long time. Three months, in fact. In response to this, the doctor had renewed the six-month section and told H he'd have to take the meds. H was very upset and tearful but acquiesced. Hence – I now see – his bad mood on the weekend. I am too stunned by this discovery to ask them why they didn't tell me any of this before. I take a sleeping pill to get a night's sleep, which, surprisingly, I do.

TUESDAY JAN 27. Alex leaves for school in (fairly) cheerful ignorance of the current crisis. Patrick rings after he's gone, and I have to tell him. He's deeply alarmed, of course. We discuss whether he should come straight home – he did that before when Henry absconded from the Ramsgate place. I say don't let's do things too hurriedly – let's wait and see.

I get a call from one Kate Collier, the missing-persons officer; am initially abrupt with her when she asks, "Is Henry with you?" – if he was, I wouldn't need to talk to her. She then asks me where he might have gone. I suggest various places, including the water meadows where we walked on Saturday. She asks, "Is there anyone he could have gone to?" I mention Peter [Henry's best friend] but add that I think that's unlikely because H dislikes using any form of wheeled transport; besides which, I don't think he knows his friend's Chichester address. And he can't have arranged to hide out there or Peter wouldn't have asked me last night for news of him.

I think of Peter not telling me what went on [Henry not taking his medication for three months] and decide that no, he's not to blame. If he had told me, I'd have had to tell the doctors. Henry would have felt betrayed by us both and it would have devastated their friendship. And Henry would have lost a friend he trusted. Friends and parents have different obligations here.

I decide that as Henry's clearly run off this time for a reason – i.e., that he doesn't want to take his meds – he's most likely hiding out with one of his friends. He knows a lot of people in Canterbury, many of them what I think of as street people – like that heroin-taking friend he spoke of on Saturday. They'd certainly sympathise with what he's doing. This thought reassures me.

Overall, I am less frantic than I feel I ought to be. Partly – mostly, really – I feel so angry with him for putting us all through this. And for being ill and impossible even if he can't help it. I feel like someone playing an unwinnable game of Snakes and Ladders – we've just painfully climbed a ladder, now we're down a bloody great snake, back at square one, goddammit.

The police have called again to ask if I can think of anywhere he might be. I've already suggested the water meadows. I remember the Saturday conversation with Henry when we were looking at the river and think with a shiver, *He couldn't have gone there, could he? Surely not, he must be with a friend*.

Surprisingly, I sleep quite well (and feel a bit guilty about that).

WEDNESDAY JAN 28. We wake up to snow on the ground – just a light covering. Enough frost to keep it there.

I don't have to teach this morning. Go to the hairdresser to have my hair done – a very overdue appointment, the roots are show-ing, but I couldn't do it at the weekend because I had that lecture to write. I'd considered cancelling today – it seems strange to be sitting there calmly when my son is missing. But I can't help Henry by not getting my hair done. As with Patrick's work, life goes on . . .

I go on to the rehab place – a Victorian mansion converted into a hospital/hostel – to talk with Michelle, the manager. Previously we've only spoken on the phone. She is kind and sympathetic and tells me a bit more about Friday's meeting, when Henry confessed he'd not been taking his meds for three months. I ask: why wasn't his blood tested before? She says it was, weekly, but only for the white blood cell count. I say, why only that? She says a bit defensively that the plasma check "isn't part of routine." (I don't ask why not, though perhaps I should.) She explains that they didn't tell me about all this because they thought Henry would do so himself. An odd assumption, since they already knew that he hadn't told me he wasn't taking the meds.

I ask to see Henry's room – it's a pleasant one at the top of the house. Not that he'll be staying there now.

I go on to my therapy session, and we talk about Henry and his disappearance. Much about his weekend visit now becomes clear, especially his very bad mood. I can now see that that silly row about the washing up was a symptom of something very wrong. So was my relief when he went – it showed how ill he really was. She [the therapist] was right to say he was too ill to be lived with. That was, in effect, what I was saying. (I can also see now that in our Saturday conversation on the water meadows about drugs – his friend giving up heroin, his own history of drug abuse in his teens, and his present abstinence from any stimulant whatsoever – Henry was really talking about his secret refusal to take the Clozaril. But he was doing it so obliquely that I didn't have a clue what he meant.)

I go back to the university and catch up with e-mail admin, marking graduate essays, seeing final-year students about their long essays, and seeing my postgraduate student.

Several calls from Patrick, who is very anxious from hearing the weather reports. He says that if Henry doesn't show up soon, he'll come back anyway.

I have Radio 3 broadcasting choral evensong on while a student comes to discuss her long essay. When it gets to the priest chanting the Collect for Safety – "Lighten our darkness, we beseech thee, O Lord, and by Thy great mercy defend us from all perils and dangers of this night" – I go quiet and say a silent prayer for Henry. Then back to talking about Oscar Wilde, my student's chosen topic.

In the office at six, I notice how quiet it is and suddenly see snow against the windowpane. I've stayed too long, I should be back home – suppose Henry might have tried to see me and found no one there? I drive back and of course the two miles take nearly an hour with poor visibility and crowded slippery roads. By the time I park the car, the sky's clearing and the moon beginning to show. No sign of Henry.

Alex comes home cheerful – there's been a huge snow fight at school. We have a good supper of steak. It's a cold night, and I wonder how Henry is. With friends in some squat, I hope.

I feel a bit drained by the anxiety and decide to have a bath and go to bed early. Am just dropping off to sleep at ten-thirty when the phone rings – it's the police to tell me my son is found, is in the Kent and Canterbury Hospital A & E being treated for hypothermia, but it's not bad and he's not thought to be in real danger. I thank them, it's a huge relief to know he's okay. (I don't add that I'm furious with him for putting us through all this anxiety.) Can't call Patrick in Iraq, so I call my sister Catherine.

Most of me would like to say "Good, he's safe" and stay in bed, but I know I must get dressed again and go out to the hospital to see him. Catherine has advised asking a friend to go with me. I think of Nicky Hallett, who, bless her, agrees at once.

I wonder whether to tell Alex it's okay, Henry's found, but his light's off and I guess he's asleep. I'll tell him in the morning. It's a cold night with a hard frost – not easy getting the car started. We get to K & C and are greeted by a surgeon who tells me cheerfully that he's been checking Henry for frostbite and it's not very bad, his feet are going pink again, so not to worry, and the hypothermia is getting better. I hadn't realised he had frostbite.

We find him hooked up to various monitors and drips, his feet in a plastic cover with air blowing through it (sounds like). He has twigs in his hair and is wearing just a hospital gown. I give him a hug and he responds but looks a bit spaced out. I ask him where are his trainers and he shakes his head; he's evidently lost them. He's in a good deal of pain from his feet, which doesn't surprise me: thawing frostbite's famously painful.

We stay with him two hours while he's transferred to one of the wards where he'll be kept overnight to check his condition. The ward feels agreeably dark and quiet after the bright A & E, though one of the patients snores very loudly. I'm glad to think H is there and not outdoors – especially when we drive back through the hard frost. I think, *Well, he* was *saved from the perils and dangers of this night,* and say an agnostic's thank-you.

THURSDAY JAN 29. Patrick rings early and I'm able to tell him Henry is safe. We share relief, and he says in that case he'll come home next week, as originally planned – it's important for our lives to go on. I feel a bit disappointed at this but don't say so – it is, after all, what we planned. I call the mental hospital and am told H is back in Amber ward, where he was before he went to rehab (it's for the less acute cases).

At five P.M. I go to see Henry, bringing some lychees and kiwi-fruit. He's very pleased to see me and enjoys the lychees. He's lying on his bed (not on the floor, as per usual) and is in a lot of pain from his feet, which are very red and swollen and tight-skinned-looking after the frostbite. He says they were unbelievably painful last night/this morning – they still hurt, but not quite so agonisingly. They look very painful.

I hold his hand and tell him how glad I am that he's safe and how grateful I am to the police that they found him. He murmurs that it wasn't the police who found him but "some people." I notice he's wearing different clothes and no trainers.

I stay an hour and then go home to supper, thinking I'd like to find out who these "people" were who helped him. I ring the missing-persons line at the police station; am told that because of the Data Protection Act, they can't say anything over the phone, but if I come to the police station, I can be told.

FRIDAY JAN 30. The cold snap is over and the snow all but gone. Now that Henry's safe, I begin to realise just how dangerous it's been for him – which I didn't really grasp while it was happening. I go to the police station and speak to Kate Collier, the missing-persons officer, who tells me what happened. Perils and dangers – they were far, far worse than I'd thought. Henry was found more than three miles from Canterbury by someone living in a cottage at Chartham, on Wednesday night, naked in the snow, apparently after having swum the river – about nine P.M. They found him and then rang the ambulance – and as they didn't know his name, the ambulance people cross-checked with the police, who had H on their missing list. They then called the rehab people, one of whom went to identify him in hospital; when that was done, they called me. That was the background to Wednesday's call at ten-forty.

These Good Samaritans obviously saved his life – it was freezing hard by nine P.M. If he'd stayed outside, he'd be dead or, at best, permanently crippled by frostbite. I am shocked by the news. I'd really like to thank these people if I knew who they were. Kate

Collier kindly says she can trace them for me and will put me in touch if they agree.

Come home and make supper for Alex and me. He talks about the Catullus he's studying, including the poem about the "bean-shaped boat" which he likes. It turns out the class has been doing Catullus's elegy for his [dead] brother this week, the one that ends *"et in perpetuum, frater, ave atque vale"* [and forever, brother, hail and farewell]. This information gives me a silent shudder.

SUNDAY FEB 1. A bright day, still blowy but with a warm west wind, everything damp and full of colour – springlike. I go to St Martin's at eleven – Henry very pleased to see me again. His feet are less swollen, though he complains again of their being numb. I give him some foot massage, which he says helps a bit.

The tabbouleh goes down well – I tell him not to eat it all, he'll have no room for lunch. He says he has a tummy bug anyway that he caught in the hospital.

After lunch I go up to the office to write a letter to the medical authorities about what's been happening. Have talked with Patrick and with my sisters (both social workers) about the failures in care – their not monitoring the blood tests to see that he was actually taking his meds, and not telling me that Henry's six-month section had been renewed, which they certainly should have done. While we don't want to pick a fight, Patrick and I agree that we mustn't let these things pass without comment. I spend an hour and a half drafting a diplomatic letter to send tomorrow, and send copies to Patrick and to my sister Teresa, asking them if it looks right. I wish Patrick were home – he will be by Thursday, but I miss him now.

At five P.M., see Henry again – I feel I owe him a double visit after not seeing him on Sat. without warning. I am worried about his saying his feet are numb – not because I think there's permanent damage from the frostbite, we've been told there's not, but because H has a long history of neglecting and damaging his feet, and if they're numb, he won't notice they hurt. I decide to speak to the nurses about this. The nurse in the office is talking on the phone.

When she's free, I mention his numb feet. She says they know about this and would like H to see a chiropodist. Henry comes up as they're saying this and they propose it. He looks shifty and won't say yes or no. Later we go back to his room, I massage Henry's feet and say a chiropodist would be a good idea. He says, "Don't want that." I say, "Why not?" He [muttering]: "Don't want them putting a bolt through my feet."

This is so absurd, I think, that I laugh. "Darling, you're bonkers! All a chiropodist would do is look at them and perhaps massage with some cream." He laughs, too, and looks reassured.

He is very warm and affectionate this afternoon. When I leave, he goes with me to the door and hugs me good-bye.

I feel tired and unwell when I get home. Turns out I have a stomach upset. I go to bed early, unable to face any food (Alex fixes his own). I throw up and have a horrible night.

MONDAY FEB 2. I wake up still ill – even getting to the loo feels like a long journey, tho' I manage to get Alex up for school – and realise I'll have to spend the day in bed. Patrick calls from Iraq – he'll be back on Friday – and endorses this.

I get a call from Kate Collier, who gives me the name (Whitcomb) and tel. no. of the people who found Henry. I call them – they're out – and leave a message.

Patrick and Teresa both call – they say my letter looks fine. Half an hour later, Mrs Whitcomb calls me and tells me the story – that at nine P.M., because their drive was deep in snow and they were expecting their son in late from work, her husband went outside to shovel and salt it. He came back saying, "There's a naked man out here," and brought in Henry. She saw he had hypothermia and wrapped him in towels and gave him a drink of water ("I knew you mustn't give hypothermia patients hot drinks"), and she stroked him and "talked nonsense to him" to keep him awake until the ambulance came. He wouldn't say where he lived – "somewhere" – and hadn't wanted to go in the ambulance. When he did, he was reciting poetry – "highbrow stuff." He'd said he'd swum the river; they weren't sure whether to believe him. Her husband had found his clothes and trainers later, several fields away from their house and near the river. They were sopping wet, but they would have been that anyway, from the thawing snow.

I thank her for saving his life, which she and her husband clearly did. She says yes, he was in a bad way and he might not have lasted the night if her husband hadn't found him. Henry asked her for an orange when in her kitchen, but not for anything else. She sounds like a very kind woman, and I'm moved by her story and her evident concern for him. I thank her again and say I'll come and get his clothes later this week. Feel like weeping, and I do.

Still feeling weak with this tummy bug. I reckon that after that awful week, my system is loudly demanding a complete day's rest. Clutch a hot-water bottle and fall into a doze.

Am wakened at three-thirty by a call from Amber ward in that deceptively casual voice, asking is Henry at home? I say no, why should he be? They tell me he's disappeared again. I ask, "Why on earth was he allowed out into the grounds?" They say he wasn't – he went out the ward door about one-thirty, they've been looking for him ever since. I say, "Oh, Jesus!" and put the phone down.

Clearly Patrick has to know this, and I phone the foreign editor at *The Independent* to pass it on. The news gets to him fast, and he calls me to say he'll be back as soon as possible. This means two days, as he first has to be driven from Baghdad to Amman in Jordan in one night, and then find a plane that'll get him to London Heathrow. The earliest he can be here is Wednesday. I also text the grim news to Daisy, Patrick's niece. I tell Alex in the evening; he appears pretty calm about it.

My insides are much better but not up to cooking, so we have a Chinese supper. The news reaches both Patrick's brothers, who phone from the US – alerted by Daisy, I think – with supportive messages.

I cannot believe the hospital has been so careless. Obviously they thought his feet were so sore, he wasn't going anywhere. But that means they were assuming he'd act like a sane person, which he's not.

I recall that exchange about his feet and his fantasy – which he must have thought real – of a bolt going through them. Realise that then I was being given a glimpse of his inner world. Or perhaps I should say, of his world, full stop. And how terrifying it is. I think of him outdoors, probably naked and all alone. I do not sleep well.

TUESDAY FEB 3. Alex goes to school. I talk with Kate Collier before I leave for work; she tells me the police are treating this as a high-risk, high-priority matter. I am a little comforted by this and by the very mild warm weather. Still, I feel near to tears all morning. I call up to cancel that seven P.M. therapy session this evening – I obviously can't leave Alex all alone and not knowing if his brother is alive or dead.

I don't post my letter to the hospital – no point, now that Henry's missing again.

Patrick rings to say he's reached Amman and will take a night plane, he'll be home tomorrow. I tell him I have a therapy session at twelve, which I'll try to go to, as I need it. But he'll be here before then, he thinks.

I am distracted with anxiety about H and near tears all the time. If he's made for the river again, God knows what will happen. After all that rain on the w/e, it's in spate. And he has nothing to eat and already has a stomach upset. I wonder, is he going to survive? Alex and I don't speak about it. How we miss Patrick.

Am haunted all night by Shakespeare's dirge "Fear no more the heat o' the sun / Nor the furious winter's rages," that I last heard spoken at the funeral of Patrick's sister Sarah. It all seems so dreadfully apposite – "The furious winter's rages" (that snow-storm), "Care no more to clothe and eat" (he doesn't), "Fear not slander, censure rash" (to him, the diagnosis of mental illness *is* that). I think again how we can trace the beginning of this horror to no one making sure he really was taking the Clozaril because testing for that "wasn't routine." It needn't have happened if the proper checks had been in place. I think, *If Henry does die out there, it'll be like the proverb about the kingdom lost "all for the want of a horseshoe nail."*

WEDNESDAY FEB 4. Both Alex and I sleep late. I take him to school and then go on to the K & C Hospital, where I have to be myself for an X-ray. I am near to tears all the time, and do break down while I'm waiting. A fellow patient looks concerned and gets me a Kleenex. I call Kate Collier, who tells me the police are getting on to the search parties with helicopters and heat sensors. I am alarmed that this hasn't been done before – how long can H last without food or clothes?

Afterwards I call Lynne Graham, Henry's social worker, who is very supportive and points out that (a) it's warm for Feb. and (b) Henry does have a track record of coming back when he breaks out like this, and seeking help – as he did from the Whitcombs. This cheers me a bit.

I want to urge the police to get on with the specialist search if they haven't already. I suppose the headquarters at Maidstone is the place to contact, but the thought unnerves me a bit – I don't know them at all. It's the kind of thing Patrick does better than me.

I spend some time searching waste ground near the hospital, the kind of place Henry likes, but realise the police will already have done this with sniffer dogs more efficiently. I go home instead and get something to eat. As I finish it, Patrick arrives, thank goodness. We share coffee and discuss how we can urge the police to get a move on. I realise that he needs briefing on what's been going on – we've not had time to talk it through, and he's not yet spoken to the police himself. He speaks to Kate Collier – and as he does, she says news is coming through of a naked male found in a back garden in Sturry. I figure that has to be Henry, and when she adds, "They're saying he looks like Jesus," I'm sure of it.

Patrick and I have lunch together, then later go to see Henry in Anselm ward. The nurses tell us that he was found naked, very dirty, covered with scratches and also with insects. (He'd slept under bushes, and the warm weather has brought all the hungry ticks out.) He's had two baths and dozens of ticks picked off him. The scratches don't look accidental; they think he's inflicted them on himself deliberately. (This has happened before, too.) He won't say where he's been or why.

They show us into his room, where he's on the bed, looking terrible. He's scratched all over – especially on his feet, his face, too – the scratches very red and sore. He looks at us with such apparent terror that I wonder if he's hallucinating. We sit down with him, Patrick with his arm round H's shoulders, I at his feet. I touch these gently and he shudders.

He weeps and grimaces silently for about ten minutes, then gradually calms down. I offer him some fruit, which he eats, and little by little he relaxes. By the end of the two hours that we stay with him, he's actually talking a little and responding, especially to Patrick. A tick which the nurse missed crawls on the sheet. Henry won't have it killed, so I catch it on a piece of pear and dispose of it out of a window (they'll open about an inch).

He complains of his feet (not surprising, they look awful) and also of a sore and horribly itchy bottom. A kind nurse comes and puts cream on the sore feet, which makes him cry out with pain, calling out nonsense syllables – these may be just shouting, but they sound to me like spells or incantations. She checks his crotch and finds he's infested there with little ticks or other bloodsucking insects; she arranges to put Derbal on it.

We reckon it's time to leave and go home, harrowed but hugely relieved. We have supper, and I start marking my current batch of essays as Patrick, exhausted after travelling for two nights, goes to bed early with a sleeping pill.

THURSDAY FEB 5. I don't want to leave Patrick alone the first day he's back, so I work at home this morning. I also write and post my thank-you letters to the Whitcombs for saving H's life, and to Kate Collier at the police station for her help. Patrick says he'll go to see Henry this afternoon and speaks to him on the phone (we're encouraged that Henry will do this). Henry asks for some "cold pea soup." I go into town and find some vegan tinned pea soup at Canterbury Whole Foods where the assistant Max knows H and asks after him. I fix this in a thermos with ice and chopped herbs for P to take in.

At six-thirty, a call from Anselm ward. A shocked and very apologetic nurse tells us H has disappeared again. They can't think how – it must have been from the yard of the ward, though the fence is supposed to be unclimbable. It can't have happened more than an hour since Patrick saw him. Patrick and I are both stunned. We can't face telling Alex yet. We go to bed and don't sleep well.

Fortunately, the weather is still mild, though blowy.

FRIDAY FEB 6. We didn't tell Alex this morning about Henry going. Couldn't entirely believe it myself. I went in to teach etc. today – found it a relief. P at home and more distraught than me.

Time goes very strangely when Henry is missing. It seems so slow, every hour one is waiting to hear news. I tell myself rationally that we're not likely to get any news for a day at least: his track record is to stay out about 48 hours. Nevertheless, every time the phone rings, I hope to hear he's found and try to disguise my disappointment that he's not.

I realise now that my warm sense of relief yesterday – Patrick home, Henry found – was based on the naive belief that this story could have a simple happy ending, like a children's book. It's not going to be like that: the best we can hope for is that the story continues. This one, I say grimly to myself, will run and run. Or at least we hope so.

While I'm at the office, one John Vatt from the police rings, saying that they've released details of Henry to the press/radio, who are interested in interviewing Patrick and me. My immediate thought is *no* – I've always loathed TV interviews with tearful parents of missing children and have no wish to weep in public for the benefit of those media vultures. I tell him the answer's probably no, but I'll confer with Patrick first.

Patrick says the key thing is, would it help H? Am rather ashamed that I hadn't thought to put that before my own pride. We agree it wouldn't – Henry won't be watching TV and won't see us, and as he's so obviously mad, any decent person who saw him would report him anyway. (As for the kind of not decent people whom I dread might find a naked H in his madness, they wouldn't be affected by seeing us on TV. But I don't say that to Patrick, and he doesn't mention it, either.) And neither of us wants to publicly attack the hospital. True, they were very careless after his first escape when they put him in the unlocked Amber ward; and obviously, they've still underestimated how high-risk he is, but they genuinely thought no one could get out. Neither they nor we realised he was as ill as he evidently is, thanks to his charm, which is still great, and his usually friendly manner.

I see my research student, catch up with e-mail. But I've done all my stuff now and am going home to join Patrick. I feel oddly dissociated. He says let's go for a drive, and we drive slowly through the lanes around Petham in the dusk, talking about Henry and Alex. We agree to tell Alex tonight or tomorrow, depending on how late he comes back. It's a great comfort to have Patrick here.

Alex returns very late because he was taking part in a school debate. His side lost, to his chagrin, but he seems to have enjoyed it. We don't mention Henry.

The sky is clear, the full moon very bright, there's frost. I wake every two hours and look out at the cold night. He'll be naked, of course. When he's like this, he's more like Edgar/Tom o' Bedlam in *King Lear* than anything else I can think of – that is, if Edgar hadn't been putting it on and really was mad.

SATURDAY FEB 7. At breakfast, I break the news of Henry's absconding to Alex before he leaves for Sat. school. Patrick makes as light of it as one can.

We sit and wait through the morning, but this time it's not a long wait. The police ring at ten-thirty to say they've found H on Canterbury golf course – naked, of course (Patrick comments wryly that at least Henry's nakedness makes him conspicuous and so shortens the police searches). He didn't go far this time. They're taking him back to St Martin's. Patrick contacts Henry's social worker, who warns us that the hospital may want to put Henry in the highest-possible-security forensic ward. This should be avoided if possible. I phone [my sister] Catherine about this; she says "forensic" = "for the criminally insane." No, we don't want Henry put there, it would be terrible for him. And there would be no justification for it except convenience – Henry's no danger to anyone except himself, he's as harmless as the toddler he sometimes resembles.

Patrick spends some time on the phone with nurses and doctors. He says the police, who are understandably fed up with having to mount repeated (and expensive) searches for Henry, have put some pressure on the hospital to put him in the most secure possible place (forensic). But the hospital has resisted this, and Henry's back in Anselm ward with the nurses he knows, on twenty-four-hour watch. Thank goodness for that.

It's obviously just as well we didn't talk to the press. If we had, the doctors would be more likely to send him to the forensic ward, and it'd be much harder for us to argue against it. All the same, we agree that I should send off a revised version of that letter to the medical staff about the failure to check on Henry and to liaise with us, which I drafted last Sunday. These matters shouldn't pass without comment.

We go to St Martin's to see Henry and reassure ourselves that he *is* in Anselm. He's sitting down there, awkwardly dressed in jeans and a shirt, not talking much but not mute, as he was on Wednesday. His feet look red and angry, but he doesn't seem as badly scratched as last time. I look out at the yard he escaped from: the metal fence couldn't be climbed but the wall could, if one were agile – it's not sheer, and there's a gutter about seven feet up that one could walk along and then jump off the end. I couldn't do it at my age, but Henry could – he's small and light, as well as being very fit and active from all the walking he does.

We talk with the nurses, who are clearly concerned for Henry – they're obviously very fond of him, despite all the trouble he's caused them.

We promise to come back and see him later. I text Alex and others to let them know he's safe, at least for now.

Patrick and I go off and have lunch at the Goods Shed, followed by a rest. Alex returns too late to join us; I fix him a *croque-monsieur*. Then we go back to see Henry. He is in his room. A kind nurse comes and asks him how he got out – she says it's important for them to know. Rather surprisingly, he tells her, and it's as I'd guessed, he climbed the yard wall and walked along the gutter. Well, at least they know now.

He's not exactly talkative with Patrick and me, but not silent, either. He gets hold of a waste bin, turns it upside down, and plays it as a drum, improvising rhymed "raps" as he's done before at bad times. "O do de do, through the hawthorn the chill wind blows" – much like that. He seems almost oblivious of us as he chants.

CHAPTER TWELVE

Patrick

Henry recovered rapidly from nearly freezing to death during his disappearances in January and February of 2004. In the following months, there were other, less dramatic escapes and attempts to escape from St Martin's. After one of these in May, he was moved to the supposedly secure ward called Dudley Venables House, which Henry, Jan, and I feared because it would be more prison-like than the rest of the hospital. Patients regarded as a danger to themselves or to others were confined there. A single-story building, it did not look very different from the outside than the other wards. The first time we went there to see Henry, a nurse asked cautiously over an intercom who we were before she opened one door, allowed us through, locked it again, and then opened an inner door which led into the main room. In front of me, I saw Henry lying half asleep on the floor, wrapped in his multicoloured Peruvian blanket. The other patients sat, mostly in silence, on the floor or on chairs in the main room. There was the sound of a television in the background. Henry said he was all right in a weak voice, but DVH struck me in those first moments as one of the most deeply depressing places I had ever been in. The place where patients socialised was a grubby smoking room, the air so full of smoke that it was difficult to breathe, the ashtrays overflowing with cigarette butts. I had been warned that violent patients were sent to DVH and looked around me with some nervousness, but then and later, I found them gentle and friendly or sometimes wholly silent, as if caught up in their own dreams. Next door to the smoking room was an "art room" where patients painted or drew and the place where Jan and I, singly or together, would normally go to talk to Henry.

Jan saw him three times a week, and Alex, despite being in a fragile emotional state himself, selflessly went to the hospital once a week. When I was in England, I could not endure sitting at home in Canterbury, thinking of him alone in that grim building, and I tried to visit him every day. We played chess and Scrabble. I asked him to teach me drawing, and he was full of praise for my awkward scrawls. I went back to Iraq thinking – wrongly, as it turned out – that at least Henry would be safer in DVH than in previous wards, and I was easier in my mind about leaving him behind. When abroad, I called him almost every day on the satellite phone and tried to say cheering things to raise his morale. Cheerfulness did not come easily, since he was in a locked mental hospital ward and I was usually inside a heavily guarded hotel in Baghdad, where there were daily bombings and shooting. Jan often had a more difficult time because Henry could sometimes be hostile to her in a way that he never was to me. He blamed her for sectioning him in 2003, though it was a joint decision, and when he was at his most psychotic, he would refuse to talk to her or would shout at her. With me, he was almost always friendly, and if he was silent at the beginning of my visit, he would start talking more or less cheerfully before the end.

We were not his only visitors. Friends and relatives from Canterbury, London, and even Ireland would go to see Henry, and he was delighted to find he was not forgotten, though he also felt bored and lonely. His mood changed unpredictably, and sometimes he sounded worryingly like a young adolescent or a child and less and less like the intelligent, quick-witted, humorous young man he had once been. We feared that his old personality was disintegrating, as we had heard from doctors could happen to people suffering from schizophrenia, symptoms including incoherence in speech and thought and inability to respond to others. But the news was not always bad. Just as we would be beginning to despair, Henry would surprise us with a flash of humour or an intelligent remark.

Conditions at DVH were particularly bad at the time Henry first went there because two patients had recently killed themselves in their rooms. Drastic measures were introduced to prevent this from happening again by making sure that, so far as was possible, the nursing staff could always observe the patients and know what they were doing. This meant that they were locked out of their bedrooms from nine A.M. until well into the evening. The rule was vigorously enforced all the time Henry was there. On being moved into DVH, he began to take risperidone, an anti-psychotic drug that could be administered via injection, so it was certain that he was receiving his medication. The risperidone was given as a so-called depot injection so it would be ingested by the patient over a period of days. Unfortunately, clozapine could not be given via injection, though the drug was demonstrably more effective than risperidone. In 1 per cent of cases when clozapine is given, patients can have an adverse reaction requiring an immediate end to treatment, which cannot be done with a depot injection. As a result, clozapine can be taken only orally, making the likelihood of noncompliance with medication much higher.

Jan and I went to see Henry a week after he had arrived at DVH and found him responding badly to the first injection. He was prone on the floor in the hallway, very woozy and in pain from muscle contractions. He clearly needed to be in bed, but when we asked, we were told he was classified as Observation 2, presumably meaning that he had to be watched by staff all the time and would not be allowed to go to bed until ten P.M. when the night staff arrived. We asked that he be allowed to go into the little garden, which was sealed off by a twelve-foot fence, but were told that the staff did not want to risk him climbing out and escaping. The distrust was mutual. Henry was not talking much to the nurses, whom he blamed for his incarceration. He looked miserable, trapped and restless, but at least he was alive and receiving treatment.

The dilemma facing us was very real. Henry was in DVH to protect him from the consequences of his psychosis. But this solution had a massive downside in that the prolonged confinement made him acutely unhappy, and this in turn exacerbated his psychosis. I sometimes used to wonder if he would not be better off wandering the countryside than being stuck in DVH, but I soon realised that if he did this, he would soon be dead. He could display great ingenuity in not taking his medication and escaping from different closed wards, but he showed little ability to survive on his own once he was free. We knew that medication would not cure Henry, but if he took the cocktail of drugs prescribed, they would keep his psychosis under control and give him a chance of returning to full sanity. His worst breakdowns and brainstorms – which he later nicknamed his "polka-dot days," though the phrase does not quite convey the terrors which then seemed to possess him – mostly struck him when he was secretly not taking the clozapine. This appeared to be the only drug strong enough to act as a barrier to bouts of madness. Jan and I found in the coming months that the injections of risperidone, in which I had originally put great faith, either lost their effectiveness over time or were never strong enough to calm Henry's mind when his mental turmoil was at its worst. During the two years he was in DVH, he switched between risperidone and clozapine without any long-term positive result. Unfortunately, Henry took a perverse pleasure in avoiding his medication, and while I suspected this, I did not realise how successful he was. The only way to get him to take the clozapine was to sit with him until he did so, which might be a matter of hours. He was able to devote more time to not taking his medication than the doctors and nurses had available to get him to take it. He was friendly to the medical staff and they liked him, but since he did not believe there was anything wrong with him or that he should be confined in a mental hospital, he saw them, at least in part, as prison wardens to be outwitted at every opportunity. I noticed that they had always won his trust rather less than they imagined, and they later felt that he had manipulated their fondness for him by covertly not taking medication, absconding, or occasionally taking cannabis. All the hospitals where Henry spent time fought hard to keep out drugs, but none wholly succeeded.

Overall, the doctors and nurses who treated Henry, and the National Health Service, did very well by him. Aside from a few weeks at the Priory, the NHS paid for all his vastly expensive treatment, even when he was in a private hospital. Burdened though Jan and I were with coping with Henry's psychosis, we did not, like American friends with similar problems, have to worry about insurance companies or what they would or would not pay for. At St Martin's, facilities were inadequate when it came to specially designed buildings for the mentally ill, especially the insecure yard, but in DVH, the doctors and most of the nurses were very good. Whatever the failings of the NHS in terms of inadequate resources or poor organisation, these problems were offset by the significant number of able and energetic staff who saw it as their vocation to look after mental patients. There were more of these admirable and committed people in DVH than in other wards because the hospital,

sensibly enough, had concentrated its best human resources to deal
with emergency or very difficult cases.

The two psychiatric consultants looking after Henry were Professor Tony Hale and Dr Bill Plummer, who wrestled tirelessly to
bring Henry's treatment-resistant schizophrenia under control and
were undismayed by repeated setbacks. They said they found Henry
"a delightful young man" who was no danger to others but had to
be confined to DVH because of "his tendency when psychotic to
abscond from the ward, wander around barefoot, swim rivers and
otherwise commune with nature, but unfortunately thereby endan-
ger himself from exposure."

From almost the first moment he was ill, Jan and I had made
repeated pleas for Henry to see a psychotherapist on a regular basis.
We knew that in general terms, psychotherapy had been down-
graded as a treatment in British and American mental hospitals over
the previous twenty years and displaced by greater reliance on medication because the utility of such therapy was difficult to prove, and
it was both labour-intensive and highly expensive. The discrediting
of R. D. Laing's theories had further undermined the role of psychotherapy. Jan and I felt that the very real benefits of medication
had been overstated; while they muted the most dramatic symptoms
of schizophrenia, they did not cure the underlying illness. Over
the last ten years, this has become a widely accepted view among
psychiatrists. Casting around desperately for anything that would
help Henry, Jan and I were probably overoptimistic in imagining
that anybody could really talk to him until he had been stabilised by
medication. Dr Plummer gently but trenchantly made the point to
us that Henry simply was not well enough to benefit from therapy
because he was too distracted and tormented by his hallucinations.
These abated at times at DVH, but they never disappeared. He was
not able to describe the forces at work in his internal world to any-

body, however sympathetic. Dr Plummer said that the only time Henry seemed to be able to think clearly was when he was doing something that required mental and physical action, such as making pottery, painting, or yoga. At such times he could hold an intelligent conversation, while at his worst he had difficulty concentrating or answering a direct question. We had suggested he receive cognitive behavioural therapy (CBT), the effectiveness of which was being increasingly recognised, but this primarily teaches people to live with their schizophrenia, and Henry's doctors said there was no evidence that it would work with somebody so acutely ill.

By the summer of 2004, Henry was as ill as he had ever been. His brainstorms seemed to come in waves, following a period when his mental clarity had improved. Neither his doctors nor we ever really understood what lay behind these surges in his psychosis. They often followed or accompanied his escapes from DVH, which he did with great frequency despite all the efforts of the staff to stop him. If a door was left open for a minute or he was given a few moments to scale the fence in the yard, he would immediately take advantage of it. A fire door left open, keys left in the lock, or a few seconds' inattention by the nurses, and he was gone. By his own count, he ran away from DVH some seventeen times over two years. Jan and I lived in fear of unexpected calls from the hospital telling us that he had disappeared. Yet again we tried to reassure ourselves by recalling that he had survived so far, and if he got into danger, he often sought help at the last moment. The reassurance was less than complete because I was convinced that Henry had survived only because of good luck.

We had moved in 2003 from our small house on Castle Street to a larger and even older house in Canterbury, at the other end of a street from Westgate, a medieval gateway in the city walls with massive twin towers. Sometimes after Henry had run away, he would come to the door late at night. Knowing this, I often sat or dozed on the sofa downstairs, hoping I would hear him knock. Several times he did turn up, and once or twice he left a note. One, which I kept in my wallet for years afterwards, read in Henry's astonishingly clear handwriting, "hope that you are not worried about me. I am eating and staying well and will stay in touch XXX Henry." Mostly, there was just a silence lasting days, until the police or the hospital called to say he had been found alive. The Kent police expressed occasional irritation that so much of their time was spent looking for Henry, but usually, they were helpful, efficient, and uncomplaining. Our hope was that Henry was not out in the fields or woods but had taken refuge with a network of friends in Canterbury, often street people, with whom he was still in contact. Sometimes this was true and his friends had fed him and given him somewhere to sleep, but too often he would be found in the countryside – cold, scratched, and half starved. But keeping him locked up was an almost equally dire alternative. In the winter of 2005–6, he spent six months without being allowed outside, even into DVH's tiny yard. This meant Henry felt he was getting less fresh air and exercise than if he had been a convicted criminal. Inadequate and insecure buildings do not excuse this. In his last months at DVH in the spring of 2006, the hospital started to rebuild the ward.

One way of satisfying Henry's understandable urge to get out of DVH was to allow him out accompanied by nurses or with us. But he wanted freedom to do what he wished without hospital or even parental supervision. He wanted to go farther than the grounds of the hospital. Henry says now that he was drawn to run away by the voices of trees and bushes, but what they told him probably reflected his own rebellious spirit and hatred for being confined. Even with a nurse on either side of him, he would suddenly take off; he disappeared so frequently that the staff at DVH refused to accompany him. Several said they could not take the responsibility or sleep at night because of worry that he would get away from them and later die in the woods or rivers around Canterbury. We thought that if he had regular visits home, he would be less likely to take off on his own. Once when Jan came to DVH to pick him up, he accompanied her through the door, made for some bushes, and stood there for two or three minutes. Jan suspected he was listening to the trees telling him what to do, because he then said, "See you later, Mum," and disappeared into Canterbury, where he was spotted by the police the same night and brought back to the hospital. Very occasionally, he would show that he retained some instinct for survival, on one occasion phoning Jan because he was having a brainstorm and had taken off his shirt outside a pub. Such moments of self-awareness were encouraging but were counterbalanced by times when he consciously or unconsciously courted danger or death.

Henry showed a dogged and touching determination to prove that he was not ill and his experience of voices and visions was real. He was entitled legally to appeal against his sectioning before a mental health review tribunal, established to prevent people from being unfairly incarcerated or persecuted. There was never any doubt what the tribunal would decide, but Jan and I came to fear these appeals, which took place every six months, because Henry was so angry and depressed after he was turned down. He himself was wholly truthful in his evidence, even when it was not in his own interest to be so frank. For instance, the proceedings of the tribunal held on September 29, 2004, record that "in giving evidence Mr Cockburn told the Tribunal that he has heard voices the previous day, the voices come from trees." Henry knew that it would be wise to keep quiet about talking trees if he wanted to persuade the tribunal to release him, but he was determined to assert the reality of his visions and voices. The tribunal members heard how he had been walking backwards, had run away three times that month, and had no insight into his illness. When his sectioning was renewed, Henry would scratch his arms, bang his head against the wall, go barefoot, refuse to wear underclothes, and then, just as we were despairing, he would rally and become calmer and more rational. When he was at his best, he produced many paintings, and some of these were exhibited at a shop in Canterbury. This was encouraging, though at first Henry had grandiose and unrealistic plans to sell them for four hundred pounds each.

We became all too familiar with these alarming mood swings, and it was clear that, after eighteen months in DVH, Henry was not getting better. On one occasion when Jan visited him at the end of 2005, she was shocked at the deterioration in his condition. He was twitching, dancing, talking gibberish, barely seemed to recognise her, and when he did so, he angrily shouted about her "getting into his head."

A sketch from 2004

Jan and I tried to think of ways by which we could break the vicious circle of partial recovery and acute relapse. By the end of 2005, we estimated that Henry had been through this cycle five times since his first breakdown, getting worse each time. The pattern was for a serious psychotic episode to be followed by slow improvement under medication over four or five months, during which we saw a gradual resurgence of concentration and creativity. And then, just at the point when his return to some sort of normal life under supervision seemed feasible, he would relapse into acute illness. We were never wholly sure what caused these relapses. It could not have been solely that he was secretly not taking his medication, because sometimes a relapse happened when he was receiving it by injection. We suspected that one cause might be that as his mind stabilised, he could see all the more clearly the misery of his own situation, his life passing him by while he was effectively imprisoned. His school friends and fellow students fell in love, had girlfriends and boyfriends, got married, and had children, while he sat on his blanket on the squalid floor of a mental hospital. The mental health tribunal had judged that one symptom of Henry's mental disorder was that he did not show insight into his illness. But its members may not have appreciated that for him, acquiring such insight was likely to be agonisingly painful. He would then see himself as living in a world that thought him mad and in which he had no prospect of happiness. No wonder he found this knowledge so unbearable that he retreated into daydreams and fantasy.

Eventually, our desire that Henry receive psychotherapy was met towards the end of 2005, though this happened only about once a month. He was seeing an excellent consultant family psychotherapist, Dr John Hills, an intelligent, realistic, and sympathetic man. Henry was probably too ill for the psychotherapy to be of much use, but Dr Hills convened meetings of all involved with Henry, mostly doctors and nurses from DVH but also his social worker, occupational therapist, and Jan and me. The aim was to develop a realistic strategy for helping him. A summary of the positive and negative aspects of his condition recognised that he was very psychotic, confused, and unable to think coherently at almost any level. On the positive side, these meetings found that he was a very engaging, courteous, gentle person whose sensitivities made him more respectful than rebellious. They thought he had a mind of high creativity and resourcefulness that, when not crossing the line into psychosis, was sharp, adroit, and original. The only part of this description of Henry's character that I doubted was the belief that he was not rebellious. On the contrary, I thought his politeness concealed a bitter sense of grievance about his incarceration, which he saw as unfair and unnecessary.

It was becoming clear by the final months of 2005 that keeping Henry pent up in DVH was creating almost as many dangers for him as it was protecting him from. He was there to keep him safe and to receive treatment, but, since he frequently ran away and spat out the most effective medication, this was not working. In addition, we did not realise at the time how much cannabis Henry was taking both inside and outside DVH. Attempts by hospital staff to isolate him only made it more likely that he would retreat into psychosis. Jan and I felt a growing sense of anger and frustration. It was decided by doctors, hospital staff, and Jan and I that Henry should be allowed out on his own with a mobile phone and under a pledge to return at a stated time. This worked, but only to a degree. I would meet Henry in town, and we would walk around Canterbury as we had once done in Brighton, often with Henry going a little faster than I could walk. I trailed behind him, frequently telling him to slow down. Being allowed out on his own made Henry a little happier, but it was nerve-racking for everybody else. Once when he was late back, a nurse rang him up, and he said he was walking along the railway tracks near a village south of Canterbury. She persuaded him to return. In another heartrending episode in early 2006, Elisa, the girl to whom he had a romantic attachment four years earlier in Brighton, came to see him at DVH. Henry had said he wanted to see her again, and Jan had located her. But when she came, Henry had gone into town to buy her a ring and had a breakdown. By the time he got back to DVH, she had gone back to London and never returned.

Letting Henry walk about by himself in Canterbury made him happier but did not do anything to reduce his underlying psychosis. By the autumn of 2005, the doctors at DVH were saying they were making little progress in treating him, and they suggested he go to the National Psychosis Unit (NPU) in south London. This was said to have the best facilities in Britain for treating people with mental disorders. Because Jan and I were near despair about Henry's future, we probably had exaggerated expectations of what the NPU could achieve, but our hopes were not unreasonable, and we were not asking for very much. We knew that the NPU, in the Bethlem Royal Hospital in Beckenham, had far more resources than DVH. Henry's living conditions would improve, more therapy would be available, and there would be specialised staff with time to make sure that he took the medication – clozapine – that did him the most good. We had heard the head of the NPU, Zerrin Atakan, praised as one of the best psychiatrists in Britain.

The failings of DVH were very evident though not the fault of the staff. Among other things, Henry was the only long-stay patient who was there for his own protection and not to protect others. I always found the other patients either friendly and shy or friendly and garrulous, but they were not always so. One night a frightened Henry rang up to say he had been attacked and punched. His doctors agreed that DVH was not the place for him. He said he would like to go to the Bethlem Royal, though not with great enthusiasm, since he still did not think he should be in any mental hospital. We had looked at some other clinics and halfway houses where psychotherapy played a larger role in treatment, but concluded that these were suitable only for those who were less ill than our son. Institutions which believed strongly in therapeutic help were not those that would keep him safe behind locked doors and insist that he take his medication.

Getting Henry into Bethlem Royal turned out to be as difficult as entering him into an elite school. He had to be assessed by psychiatrists from the NPU, and they normally suggested changes in treatment before a patient was admitted. Finally, the NPU agreed in general terms to take Henry, and we expected a carefully organised transition period. Instead – rather bizarrely, given his delicate mental state – he was transferred there with only a few hours' notice in May 2006. Jan was all in favour of Henry being moved but had forebodings that the move was all too swift, disorienting for him, and he would feel more isolated away from Canterbury, where, even at his most psychotic, he had a circle of friends. He himself had doubts at the last minute. When Jan came to see him at the Bethlem Royal on the evening of the day he arrived there, he confided, "I shouldn't have come here. The trees were angry with me when I left."

Chapter Thirteen

Henry

It was at St Martin's that I began to have what I now call "the torments" or my "polka-dot days." They can happen at any time, day or night. Usually, I see rings, like the rings you see in a jewellery shop. Every hollow in a tree, every piece of ivy, all look like they're turning into rings. Not a moment's pause; rings everywhere. I get this feeling of inner torment that I am a sinner and that I will die or be physically tortured. I feel that I am being drained into a dark, godless world and I pray to God that it will stop. I am tormented by forces that usher me hither and thither. "Don't go in there," they say, "come nearer." I hear the seagulls call.

The first time this happened was when I was first sectioned and I was in Anselm ward. I was invited to a play at the Marlowe Theatre in Canterbury by one of the hospital staff. I walked there from St Martin's, about a mile and a half away. The night before I had spent sitting in the bathtub thinking nasty thoughts. In my head, I had been calling my friend Keeva a "nigga" and saying that another one of my friends, a girl, had a penis. I had been sitting there imagining that a girl I fancied had dropped her trousers down in full public view. I was thinking vicious nasty thoughts.

Just before I got to the Marlowe Theatre, a car went past. The rumbling of its engine seemed to be telling me to run away and not go to the theatre, but I went along anyway and watched the play. I remember looking at the play cynically, and when I was at my most cynical, one of the actors said, "Someone in here has very thick skin." I walked out of the theatre and there was a little robin on the step. It seemed to be telling me that it wasn't so bad that I had gone to the theatre and there wasn't much else I could have done. So I jumped over a fence and thought I should make a run for it, but I didn't have the courage. I went back into the theatre and looked at all the binoculars on the backs of the chairs. I wanted them to smile at me.

That was when things started to get bad for me. I saw people outside the theatre looking for sponsors for a charity. They asked someone if he wanted to join, and the person firmly said no. It was as if I myself had done a terrible thing: I had unleashed a terrible aura onto the street. I walked back to my parents' house, and it was like the world was caving in on me. I'd look at the floor of the house and see every little dot on the floor. There wasn't much my mother could do to console me. I went into the kitchen and could hear the girl in my head saying, "What do you want? I don't love you." My brother, Alex, decided to walk me back to the hospital, and things went from bad to worse. As we were walking, I decided I should have run off earlier in the day outside the theatre. We went near the cinema, and I climbed into the back of a garden. The scar that runs over my heart, which I got from jumping over a barbed-wire fence in Scotland when I was about ten, started to come up again. The garden which we were in was full of birds who weren't tweeting but were cawing at me, the sort of noise crows make. It was an unpleasant mocking noise. I got

on my knees and kept repeating the lines of a Lauryn Hill song that
sounded like:

Every man get on his knees and repent,
Can't slip-talk on the day of judgement.

   My brother walked me back to the hospital, and I stayed in the
room of another patient called Rob. I began to feel a little bit better
when the nurses made me go back to my room. The feeling didn't
leave me for about a week. It was a bitter week for me. I truly thought
I was going to die.

The "polka dots" often returned in the years that followed. At their
worst, they would last half a day and at best about three hours. I
would imagine that everybody could read my thoughts. I was full
of guilt that I was a closet gay, a racist, and generally evil. I would
say irrational things like "Does God believe in me?" and think I was
being evil by the way I phrased it, making it sound as if I were more
powerful than God. When I was in the depths of despair, I would
recite the Lord's Prayer to comfort myself:

Our Father who art in heaven,
Hallowed be thy name.
Thy kingdom come. Thy will be done,
On earth as it is in heaven.
Give us this day our daily bread.
And forgive us our trespasses,
as we forgive those who trespass against us.
And lead us not into temptation

but deliver us from evil.
For thine is the kingdom,
the power, and the glory,
forever and ever. Amen.

This prayer would give me some comfort, but I would always stop reciting in the middle, where it says, "Forgive us our trespasses as we forgive those that trespass against us," because I would think of my own trespasses and of those that trespassed against me. Usually, I thought I was committing a sin by thinking people were trespassing against me.

Two years after I first had a "polka-dot" day, I had a particularly bad attack. I was still at DVH, but the plan was for me to go to the Bethlem Royal Hospital in south London, which I said at first was all right by me, though later, I changed my mind. One day the torments returned after I had got in touch with Elisa, the girl I had fancied from Brighton, and invited her down to visit me. From then on things went from bad to worse. I decided I needed to buy her a wedding ring, so I wandered into town. By this time I was being allowed out on my own. Everything I did seemed wrong. I had only ten pounds on me, and I went to buy a custard tart and left the money in the shop. I kept looking for coins on the floor. I saw rings everywhere. I thought I was being tricked into finding the dark ring of Sauron, the demonic overlord in Tolkien's *The Lord of the Rings*, and that I myself was evil. I managed to scrounge ten pounds off a friend's dad whom I met on the street, but by then the jewellery shop was closed. I walked along the riverbank thinking I would never see daylight again. I jumped off a bridge into the river, hoping to kill myself. I waded my way across the river and got up the bank and made my way into town. I thought I was Gollum, also from *The Lord of the Rings,* that I was a sinner and was subservient to the dark ring. Somehow I had it on my finger, and I had become invisible and no one could see me. I tried to choke myself on my own tongue. Then I saw a woman walking towards me. I asked her if she could see me, and she said yes, she could see me. I found myself walking towards the police station; I was soaking wet. The police took me back to DVH, where Elisa had left. I did buy a wedding ring in the end, but later, I threw it away. Elisa never came to visit me again.

I did not look at my medication as a way of preventing the polka dots. My attitude to it was the same as my attitude to hospitals in general: that there was nothing wrong with me, I had no real say in what happened to me, and I was being dealt with unjustly. I would put the tablets between my lip and my front teeth and pretend to swallow them. I was suspicious of the tablets and wanted to know what they were made out of. The doctor said they were synthetic, made out of molecules. This didn't mean much to me. I wanted to know if they were organic – made out of plants or minerals. I suspected they were made out of human parts. The medication, clozapine, made me very drowsy, and I developed a rash on my belly as a side effect. I would try my hardest not to take it. One day I found a pamphlet in the hospital about this boy who had been saved by the drug. I ripped the paper in two and put it in the bin. I wanted to live life to the fullest and felt that taking the medication would hinder me.

I dreamt of running away and took every opportunity to do so. At the same time, I found something attractive about DVH. It wasn't the sort of place you could take a baby, but it had a community spirit, and the staff shared in this. I met everybody from humble Christians to outright criminals there, and I didn't feel lonely. We often had occupational therapy, and Leonie, the occupational therapist, arranged cooking, art therapy, music therapy, a music group, and current affairs. On Mondays we had a newspaper group which looked at the newspapers and ate muffins. I asked her if it was all right to do graffiti as a mural on the wall of the yard, and she said

no. I asked if she could ask Dudley Venables, the vicar after whom
DVH was named and who was slowly dying in a hospital, whether
it was all right to do graffiti. The answer came back a firm no, but
Leonie suggested that I do graffiti on a wall outside the DVH garden.
We got paints but could not use spray paints because of the fumes.
First we painted the wall white, and then I painted the letters DVH on
the wall in green with a black outline. It wasn't my greatest painting, but it looked better than the grim brick wall underneath. I read
some books, including *The Arabian Nights* and half of *The Prophet*
by Kahlil Gibran. This inspired me to do a couple of drawings of
people in boats on a placid sea (*The Prophet* is a book about a man
who leaves his hometown to sail the wide ocean).

I was visited by family and friends pretty regularly at DVH, as the
hospital was close to the home where I had grown up. Many visitors
were my old friends from Canterbury whom I had known during my
dope-head days. None of my friends from college ever came to see me.
Once my cousin Chloe came to visit me – she is a tall American who had
long brown dreadlocks, as I did at that time. We compared our dreadlocks, and she said that the hair on the back of my head had become
so matted that it formed a single lock. She was an artist in New York.
We talked about a spiderweb on the wall of DVH which seemed to be
pointing west. After talking to Chloe and looking at the web, I felt an
inspiration to go west, over the Atlantic to New York, Cuba, Jamaica,
and the Amazon. Earlier I had made plans to go down the River Stour
from Canterbury to Ramsgate with the other patients, and there, on
a little offshore ridge I knew, I would make a bigger boat and sail to
London. Then we would sail to Paris along the Seine, down into the
Mediterranean to Jerusalem, and from there to either Africa or India.
But Chloe and the spiderweb made me think I ought to go west instead.

Aside from my family, the person who visited me the most was
Virginia Keane. She knew me as a teenager before I was hospitalised,

and she knew my father from when they were both children in Ireland. Many years ago she had cancer of the jaw and had a bit of her hip removed and inserted into her jaw. This did not stop her travelling, and she divided her time between her house in Ireland and going to Ethiopia in Africa and Rajasthan in India. The one good thing about being in the hospital is that I became much closer to her. She visited me in Canterbury and Ramsgate and all the other hospitals I was in.

Once I had a strange meeting with her. At the time I was running away from DVH very often. One day I climbed over a twelve-foot fence, went into a swamp, and came out with my trousers wet, though they were soon dried by the summer sun. I met a kid at the bus stop who couldn't have been older than thirteen or fourteen. I gave him a piece of advice: "If you ever meet a psychiatrist, don't confess to anything." The next thing I knew there were all these kids from a nearby housing estate following me, shouting "Weirdo" and "Get back to the hospital." I came to the fence dividing the housing estate from St Martin's, which has big grounds. The wind was ushering me towards the fence, but I couldn't understand why the wind wanted me to go back towards the hospital. One of the kids pointed to the fence and said, "You can get over that way." I jumped over the fence and walked through the hospital grounds and out the other side past an army barracks. Suddenly, a taxi pulled up, and Virginia got out and gave me a big hug. It turned out she had come to visit me in DVH and found me not there. I realised the reason why the wind had blown me over the fence between the estate and the hospital was so that my meeting with Virginia could take place. She persuaded me to get in the cab and go to my parents' house. We went as far as the cinema, and I talked her into going into a clothes shop because I looked like a street rat. Eventually, I walked to my parents' house. I picked some flowers along the way to give them. They were pleased to see me but told me to go back to the hospital.

It was finally decided that I should go from DVH to the Bethlem Royal, a hospital in London. The day I went there did not go well. I walked out of DVH, accompanied by two members of the staff towards the car that was to take us there. I heard two birds call to me to run away, but I didn't have the stomach to do it. I closed my eyes during the whole journey to the Bethlem Royal, and when I opened them, we were on the grounds of the hospital. After a search, we found Fitzmary 2 ward, which was to be my new home. I saw a few faces that I had known in Canterbury: a black girl called Allison and a white man named Andy, but he left the day I arrived. Once in the ward, I went straight to the smoking room, where there was an old man with teeth yellow from smoking too much and a black man called Rob. I scrounged cigarettes off the two of them. The hospital staff wouldn't allow me to go out of the building for three days because they wanted to monitor me. I wanted to go to church – I was becoming deeply religious – so the local vicar came to see me. I don't think I told him all my problems. The main advantage in going to Fitzmary 2 was that my room was open to me twenty-four hours a day.

Henry with Virginia Keane in the hospital, 2006

The next night I was in my room when it struck me that I was in a strange place where I knew hardly anybody. I started reading Tolkien's *The Lord of the Rings*, which turned out to be a bad idea. The polka dots hit me, and I threw the wedding ring that I had bought Elisa out the window. I thought I was turning into Gollum, who is a sort of goblin. If the windows of Fitzmary 2 hadn't been sealed tight to prevent people from opening them and absconding, I probably would have jumped out headfirst and shattered my skull. I felt terrible, and this feeling lasted until the next morning, when I saw images on the wall. When I did get to go out for a walk, a nurse and I walked around the grounds in the drizzle. A few days later, I went to the church, and afterwards I sat in the sun talking to a number of reformed alcoholics. There was a swimming pool on the grounds of the hospital that I would use, and I occasionally played basketball in the sports hall. All the same, I don't think there was one second at the Bethlem Royal when I did not want to run away.

Chapter Fourteen
Patrick

The Bethlem Royal psychiatric hospital in south London had its origins 750 years ago in the centre of the city; its reputation for housing the violently insane was the origin of the word "bedlam." It is today the largest centre for the treatment of schizophrenia in Europe, while one of its sections, the National Psychosis Unit, specialises in caring for patients who are not responding to treatment. Situated in what were once the extensive grounds of a private mansion in the well-to-do London suburb of Beckenham, Bethlem Royal's wards and workshops are surrounded by attractive parkland. Henry's ward was called Fitzmary 2 and was on the second floor of a two-storied building in front of which was an area of open grass and a small stretch of woodland. We were pleased to find that the ward was larger and better equipped than DVH in Canterbury. Patients had bigger bedrooms, a canteen serving tolerable food, a reading and television room with large windows, and a smaller room for smoking.

The doctor in charge was Zerrin Atakan, a consultant psychiatrist of whom we had heard nothing but praise from other psychiatrists who worked with her. She had long experience of acute mental ill-ness, had researched the link between cannabis and psychosis, and had been headhunted by the National Health Service to run the NPU. Born in Turkey, she had once been a singer in a music group and was a talented painter as well. She stayed in Britain because she was blacklisted by military regimes from working in her own coun-try despite her stellar professional reputation. Jan and I thought her high intelligence, artistic temperament, and slightly dissident back-ground might enable her to achieve a rapport with Henry, who gen-erally regarded his doctors and nurses with rather more resentment and reserve than they imagined, holding them responsible for his unjust confinement.

Sadly, our cautious hopes were disappointed over the eight months Henry was at the Bethlem Royal between May 2006 and January 2007. This lack of progress was not Dr Atakan's fault but stemmed primarily from the intractable nature of Henry's illness combined with unexpected institutional failings. To our growing dismay, our experience left us feeling that the hospital was poorly organised, staffed by good-hearted people but without clear priori-ties in its treatment of those with serious mental disorders.

Henry's change of hospitals did not go well from the beginning. His transfer was too sudden, and he found the shift stressful and upsetting. A bed in Fitzmary 2 had unexpectedly become available, and Henry learned that he was leaving DVH only a few hours before his departure. We had originally suggested that the move from Can-terbury to London be more carefully prepared, but we changed our minds because we feared Henry might lose his place. His own memo-ries of DVH strike me as overly rosy and nostalgic, but for all its failings, the grim-looking ward he lived in for over two years had a more communal and villagelike atmosphere than the outwardly more attractive but aseptic facilities he was moving to. The patients in DVH came mostly from Canterbury and east Kent and often knew one another before they were sectioned. Communal solidarity was important for Henry, who had spent almost all his life in Canterbury and was always highly sociable and reliant on a large circle of friends. When he and I were walking around Canterbury during his last months at DVH, our progress was slow because he greeted and spoke to people he knew every few hundred yards. Now, at the Bethlem Royal, there were no familiar streets, and he felt isolated because he knew almost nobody inside or outside the hospital. The atmosphere was distantly friendly but also struck me as chill and institutional, and I was worried when I noticed that other patients were silent and self-absorbed, seldom talking to each other or to Henry. There appeared to be a high turnover of senior nurses, so Jan and I found it difficult to speak to anybody who, however sympathetic, had worked with Henry for longer than a couple of months and could discuss disturbing signs that his condition was getting worse rather than better.

A month after he arrived, Henry was becoming increasingly anxious and depressed and was beset by tormenting ideas as well as hallucinations and voices. What he imagined or daydreamed had the frighteningly vivid reality of a nightmare that would not go away and from which he could not easily wake. A feature of his psychosis was that he often felt a deep sense of guilt over trivial incidents that were not his fault, or over making the wrong decision about something insignificant. At the same time – and this was true for most of his long years in mental hospitals – Henry, except when he was at his most psychotic, could act perfectly sane. During his time at the Bethlem Royal, he and I had picnics on a blanket on the lawn under the trees in the park and chatted away merrily before going for walks on the pretty, well-maintained, but rather desolate hospital grounds. Once in the evening, after we had been picnicking, he phoned me at home and said mournfully, "I am feeling low. I feel that I am turning into Gollum in *The Lord of the Rings*."

I was making sympathetic noises about things getting better in the long term when Henry abruptly changed conversational gear and made a purely practical request: "Could you get me flip-flop sandals because my shoes are hurting me." This exchange was typical of the way his mind would flit between the imaginary and the real.

In weeks leading up to Christmas 2006, Henry was becoming more frustrated, and Jan and I were increasingly worried. She talked to him about persuading the ward staff to give him more freedom. "They won't listen," he replied. "They never do."

Jan did not think this was really true, but it reflected how Henry was feeling. She complained to Dr Atakan that his treatment had become focussed on stopping him from running away. He had been kept under one-to-one observation by a nurse for three or four weeks, with his smallest action noted down. Jan said, "This isn't helping him recover, because it is making him feel even more trapped and even more irritable. He is lonely and isn't part of any group doing music, art, pottery, or drama, though he plays his guitar a good deal. I don't think he has made many friends with fellow patients, though there are some nurses he gets on with well enough. What he really likes doing is socialising with the patients in the ground-floor ward when he goes into the garden, but the ward managers don't like him chatting and drinking tea there."

The staff at Bethlem Royal could see Henry was not getting better but were baffled about what to do. The biggest disappointment at the hospital was that Henry did not use the gym, go swimming, or even paint very much. We had hoped he would make greater use of the better facilities, but their use was often prevented by bureaucratic obstacles. We had been warned about this by an occupational therapist at DVH, who worked at the Bethlem Royal some years earlier and had cautioned us against overoptimism about how much good the place would do Henry. She said that it had "lots of equipment and patients who would like to use it, but it doesn't bring them into contact very often." We had not taken this advice seriously enough because we were eager to convince ourselves that the hospital might be a turning point in Henry's treatment. The warning turned out to be all too true. For instance, there was a gardening group for patients, but health and safety officials at the hospital vetoed any digging because, so we were told, they feared that tools such as rakes and shovels might be dangerous in the hands of sectioned patients. So far as we could judge, the attitude of hospital administrators was a self-defeating mixture of overcaution in small matters and lack of vigour in important ones. Though Henry was banned from meeting people in another ward, oversight to prevent him leaving the hospital was surprisingly ineffective. To escape from Fitzmary 2, Henry had only to get through two locked but flimsy doors, which were not always locked, go down two short flights of stairs, and pass through an unlocked and unguarded front door. Dr Atakan, who in 2007 resigned in frustration at her lack of full authority over the National Psychosis Unit, says that she had to struggle with hospital officials' resistance to locking the outer doors of the ward. We had learned the hard way that a degree of restraint was essential if Henry was to receive treatment in a secure place that he could not easily leave when the trees told him to take flight or he had one of his terrifying brainstorms.

A second disappointment was equally serious: we assumed that the staff at Fitzmary 2, more numerous and better trained than at DVH, would be able to persuade him to take the clozapine. But a test in December, about five months after he had moved to the Bethlem Royal, showed that there was no sign of clozapine in his blood. He must have successfully avoided swallowing his pills and was spitting them out later or, if he did swallow them, he must have been deliberately vomiting them up. Bethlem Royal, for all its high reputation for treating schizophrenia, was failing just as much as ill-equipped DVH to meet Henry's most vital needs: to keep him safe and to ensure that he took his medication, which were, after all, the reasons he was confined in a mental hospital in the first place.

Jan and I were inured to disappointment by this time, but Bethlem Royal's high reputation made the blow harder when it failed to do Henry much good. We racked our brains trying to think what else we could do to help him, but we had no alternative plan and could only hope something would turn up.

The facilities at DVH were so poor and supervision of patients at the Bethlem Royal so lax partly because of radical changes in the way the mentally ill have been treated in Britain, Western Europe, and the US over the last half century. Health experts increasingly see some of these developments – however well meant at the time – as a catastrophic setback in the care of those with mental disorders. Henry suffered from this revolution in mental health care, and mistakes were made in his treatment, but he was also looked after by dedicated and highly skilled doctors and nurses and was less seriously affected than many others. He was lucky to come from East Kent, where provision for the mentally ill has a reputation for being better organised and implemented than in much of Britain. The East Kent Mental Health Trust unstintingly sought effective treatment for him despite many setbacks. Even so, the options available to officials of the trust were largely determined by the fact that the old system of mental asylums, built in Victorian times and in the first half of the twentieth century, has been mostly dismantled over the last fifty years, and too little has been done to replace it. Prisonlike many of the old asylums may have been, but at least they were a haven for people too mentally ill to find work, food, and shelter for themselves. Inside their walls, life may have been institutionalised, but one could safely behave bizarrely or even madly without derision or persecution. Certainly the alternative to the mental asylums has generally proved worse than what went before. In Britain this went under the attractive-sounding name of "care in the community," which must be one of the most deceptive and hypocritical phrases ever devised by a government. It was claimed at the time that big psychiatric hospitals would be replaced by a network of outpatient clinics, halfway houses, and hostels overseen by specialist psychiatrists, doctors, and nurses. In reality, British Health Minister John Hutton said in 1999 "the present system of care in the community has actually become 'couldn't care less' in the community."

As asylums closed en masse in the 1980s, those who once found a measure of protection in them had nowhere to go and were sometimes thrown onto the streets, becoming "sidewalk psychotics"; were sent to prison; or, more usually, were looked after by their overburdened families. Between the 1950s and today, the number of beds available to psychiatric patients in Britain fell from 150,000 to 30,000. In the US a similar shutdown of mental asylums was presented as "deinstitutionalisation," a word which has a fine libertarian ring to it until one realises that many people with mental problems have a desperate need for an institution to protect and look after them. In the US the number of beds available for psychiatric patients in public hospitals fell 90 per cent, from 558,000 in 1955 to 53,000 in 2005. Many patients became homeless and were dealt with by the police rather than by health workers. An expert report on the shortage of hospital beds for the mentally ill notes sardonically that the three largest de facto psychiatric institutions in the US today are the Los Angeles County jail, Chicago's Cook County jail, and New York's Rikers Island. The worst of the old asylums may have been hellholes, but the response should have been their improvement, not their abolition.

The British detective-story writer P. D. James, who worked as an administrator in the British National Health Service in London when "care in the community" was being introduced and whose husband was a long-term patient in a mental hospital, comments bitterly that community care "could be described more accurately as the absence of care in a community still largely resentful or frightened of mental illness." The policy greatly deepened the anxiety of families, who often have to rely on their own very limited resources to look after a mentally ill relative. Jan and I were able to find a bed in a mental hospital for Henry easily only because he was so acutely psychotic that there was no doubt about his being sectioned. Sectioning by a doctor meant that a hospital had to find room for him, while people who are only a little less sick are sometimes not sectioned because doctors know there are too few resources to treat them. Twenty years earlier, there would have been no such problem in Canterbury, because just to the west of the city was a mental hospital called St Augustine's. It had beds for two thousand patients as well as specialised education units for adolescents and adults with mental disorders. But by the time Henry became ill, the hospital had been closed down and its grounds sold off for a housing development.

Even now the cruelty and unnecessary misery stemming from the dissolution of the mental asylums in the years after World War II is astonishing. That it happened with so few public protests, perhaps because the victims could not speak up for themselves and were regarded with dread by the wider public, is a surprise and a shame. The public went along with the closures because some hospitals were very bad, and even those which were good had wards where insane people were confined in appalling conditions. As these psychiatric hospitals came under attack, it was easy to demonise them as the dumping grounds for people who had breached social conventions of the day, such as girls with illegitimate children. In addition, medical staff had used electric shock treatment, which was traumatic for patients and showed little benefit. And movies like *One Flew Over the Cuckoo's Nest* reinforced the perception that such institutions were prison camps misruled by authoritarian monsters.

Mental asylums became the targets of criticism from an odd but influential coalition of civil-rights liberals and fiscal conservatives. Radicals like R. D. Laing argued that people with mental disorders were the victims of their families and could be better treated outside mental hospitals. The so-called father of community care in Britain in the early 1960s was the right-wing libertarian Conservative health minister Enoch Powell, later notorious for his attacks on immigrants and immigration. The big psychiatric hospitals had few defenders. Governments and health officials eager to save money made common cause with liberals and the left, who saw mental patients as prisoners unjustly incarcerated. In reality, no group of people is more vulnerable or less likely to be tolerated – still less cared for – by a public viscerally frightened of madness. An important motive for closing down the big asylums was expense. Mental health care is costly; many people at hospitals like St Augustine's in Canterbury were incurable, there for life. At one facility for accommodating, treating, and educating mentally disordered adolescents, also near Canterbury, costs per patient in the 1980s were five times the fees of Eton, Britain's most aristocratic boarding school.

Not all the motives for closing down the mental asylums were mercenary or mistaken. People might often be ignorant of how the mentally ill were treated, but they had a vague sense of guilt that patients had been hard done by in the past. Warders at the original "Bedlam" – the modern successor of which is Bethlem Royal –

had been notorious in the eighteenth century for making money by charging visitors in search of amusement to watch the mad antics and delusions of patients. When I was a boy in the 1950s, psychiatric hospitals were familiarly called "loony bins," a phrase evoking images of padded cells and straitjackets.

Getting rid of this system began to appear all the more feasible in the mid-1950s thanks to the discovery of effective anti-psychotic drugs. These could usually control the most exotic and dramatic hallucinations and voices, though they were less successful in dealing with passive symptoms such as apathy and inability to relate to others. By the late 1970s and early 1980s, the use of depot injections, whereby the drug gradually disperses into the bloodstream, meant that some but not all medication could be administered by a nurse once a fortnight. This made compliance with the medication automatic and appeared to make it unnecessary for a mentally ill person to be resident in a hospital or even to see a doctor frequently. Though depot injections made treatment easier and more certain, psychiatrists overestimated what such medication could achieve. Their perceptions were reinforced by research funded by pharmaceutical companies, which put medication at the centre of all treatment and downplayed therapy and the beneficial impact of an improved environment.

As the old mental asylums closed, care in the community could have worked only if it had been sustained by a network of psychiatrists, social workers, and clinics. This system never existed and was never likely to be created because it would have high costs and governments had closed the asylums partly to save money. Public protest over what had been done was limited. The one time the public appeared to wake up and become conscious of the inadequacy of the new arrangements for the mentally ill was when there was a spectacular murder by a person with mental health problems. There are at least fifty such murders in England every year, though more people are murdered by drunks than by the mentally ill. When there is a murder by a mentally ill person, there is often a brief and usually ill-informed debate on why a potential killer had not been hospitalised and was on the loose despite many warning signs. Some who later committed murder had vainly sought to get themselves admitted to a hospital only to be told that there were no beds available. An unfortunate effect of such episodes is to reinforce the pariah status of those with mental disorders and to scapegoat doctors and social workers for not sending potentially dangerous people to mental hospitals, ignoring the fact that these institutions are now few and far between.

Fear of madness and the mad is probably less than it was, and campaigners for the mentally ill congratulate themselves on reducing stigma. But fear of those believed to be insane was one reason the Victorians allocated so many resources to building mental asylums. A schizophrenic patient is a hundred times more likely to kill him- or herself than to kill somebody else. But the connection between schizophrenia and violence is a little stronger than is openly admitted by many psychiatrists. About 8 per cent of offenders who murder or attempt a murder have schizophrenia, and schizophrenic patients are four times more likely to be involved in violent incidents than people who have not been diagnosed as having a psychosis. An indication of how care in the community has, in practise, meant abandoning the mentally ill to their own devices is that the majority of schizophrenic offenders in Britain were known to the psychiatric services but were not receiving treatment at the time of their offence. Reducing the stigma and ignorance surrounding mental illness is beneficial, but it risks undercutting the case that those suffering from it desperately need expensive special treatment and facilities.

Henry was never in danger of being thrown onto the street or not getting a bed in a psychiatric hospital. But he was affected in other ways by the destruction of the old asylum system in that there were now so few places that could keep him secure while treating him. To do so effectively implied a degree of restraint and protection that was long out of fashion. It is true that there were people in the old psychiatric hospitals who suffered more from incarceration than they gained from institutional care. But there were others like Henry, who really did need to be looked after twenty-four hours a day. For long periods Henry ended up getting the worst of all possible worlds. He was not allowed even limited liberty because the wards he was living in were not built to allow it and also prevent him from absconding. He complained that he was worse off than a prisoner in jail, who at least had a yard to walk in. And still staff failed to stop him from periodically escaping or not taking his medication. It seemed that they were never going to bring his psychosis under control.

Chapter Fifteen
Patrick and Henry

The most significant episode during Henry's months at Bethlem Royal, which frightened me more than his previous disappearances, happened in August 2006, when Jan, Alex, and I went to what had been my parents' house in Ireland for a holiday. A few days after we arrived, I got a phone call from the hospital saying that Henry had broken through two doors and run off. He had left the hospital several times but only for brief periods. This was evidently more serious, because he had disappeared in London which, unlike little Canterbury, was a vast city that he did not know well. Henry later explained that he had phoned Elisa in Brighton, and a man with a husky voice had answered. Enraged, he smashed open the hospital doors – less difficult than it sounds because both had flimsy locks – and fled. He walked to the local station and took a train to central London, where he stayed in the apartment of a girl he had been to school with. He phoned his friend Peter in Canterbury, who came up to London with his girlfriend, Françoise, the following morning. Henry's account of what happened is similar to his previous wanderings, except this time he was penniless and half starved, and his visions and paranoia seem to have taken over his mind more completely than ever:

My friends from Canterbury came around midmorning. The sky was blue and we went for a walk, but suddenly, I felt I was in danger, so I jumped over a large wall into a school. I walked into the school building to find a black guy at a desk. I asked if I could give the kids an art lesson, and he said no. I jumped over another wall and found myself in a thicket beside a railway line. I thought I was being followed and ran into a block of flats. As I went up the stairs, I met lots of Arab children, and my heart was beating rapidly as I hid in an alcove at the top. I could hear helicopters not far away and the children trying to distract them. I thought I was close to death, but finally, the helicopters moved away, and as I came out of the alcove, the children whom I had passed on the stairway were nowhere to be seen.

I found my friends not far away. I walked with Peter into a Chinese shop to make it more difficult for anybody to follow me. Peter got his guitar, and we took the underground into central London, where we walked over a bridge across the Thames. We sat on the bank of the river playing Bob Marley, and I felt a force pulling me into the Thames, but I resisted it and didn't jump in. The tide was going out and we went down some stairs and sat on a stretch of sand. A nice woman said there was going to be a concert on the sand later, and I saw the water lapping on the shore. I said, "Move back, move back, sea." A man whom I think was dealing heroin shouted "Fuck off" at me. We walked to a place where there were skateboarders, and I saw a red bus crossing the Thames and felt I should have been on that bus. A girl with a Russian accent asked to take a picture of us, and again I felt paranoid. We were in Charing Cross, and everybody seemed to be looking at us, and I pulled a stupid face when she took the picture.

We jumped on a train to Brighton and got off without paying. Peter, Françoise, and I went to a squat where there was another friend of mine called Michael. The squat was full of all sorts of junk such as old saws and knives. They were boiling up some form of opiate, and I tasted a spoonful of it. The people there were playing a guitar, and Michael, with whom I shared a deep religious belief, started speaking in tongues. I lit a candle and tried to teach Peter yoga, which I had been doing for two and a half years. Night fell, and we went outside and walked through the dark streets. We came across a massive wall with vines clinging to it, and I decided to climb it, though it only just took my weight. I climbed up about forty feet, and as I reached the top, I felt a stone come loose under my foot and fall to the ground. On the other side was a Jewish cemetery, and I stayed the night there, thankful for the rest. The next morning I climbed down out of the cemetery and found myself in somebody's back garden. I heard a voice telling me to go into a house and steal something, but I couldn't pluck up the courage to do it. An angry woman came out of the house and told me not to come back.

I felt in my pocket and found I had about three pounds. I hid in the courtyard of a hotel. I heard a policeman walk past, and after a while I left. Everybody appeared to know me, and a van stopped near me and the driver said, "All right, Cockburn." I hid in the bushes beside the road until midnight. A badger walked up to me, but I raised my fist and it disappeared. I felt guilty because maybe the badger would have helped me keep warm. I became more paranoid and decided to move away into some heavy undergrowth, but I could see torches in the mist. I decided to bolt for it and ran down a side street into a car park, over several walls through people's gardens, and under an outdoor staircase that had a tomato plant over it. Dawn rose, but I was famished after not having eaten for a couple of days. I took a leaf from a tomato plant and ate it, but it didn't fill me up. Then, strangely, I believed that my cousin's daughter – little baby Maya – was in my arms and that I had to keep her silent or somebody would come along and kill the two of us. There was a blue tarpaulin that I hid under. It rained, heavy tropical rain which fell on the tarpaulin, and I drank the beautiful water, which quenched my thirst completely. Later, I found a tangerine on the road that I thought somebody had left for a seagull. I was so hungry that I ate it myself and walked back to the house with the tomato plant on its staircase. As I sat there, I thought of my aunt who lives in Cardiff, and I climbed through a window and into a house. The owner, a big redheaded man with a beard, saw me and punched me in the face. I said I was only looking for my aunt, and he said, "Oh," and I went out of his garden and over the fence. I was still thinking of my aunt and thought I was in Cardiff in the 1970s. I was looking for a mental hospital because I was tired and weary.

Significantly, in the middle of his delusion about being in Cardiff in another era, Henry thought of a mental hospital as a place of refuge. Otherwise, his psychosis was very deep and all-consuming. A sign of this is that he abandoned Peter – who was his closest friend and had come with him to Brighton – without a qualm when he climbed up the forty-foot wall and passed the night in a cemetery. Writing in 2009, three years after these events, Henry recognises that his fears were paranoid but still half believes in the reality of his experiences.

I walked around not knowing where I was until I realised that I was not in Cardiff and it was not the 1970s. I begged a cigarette off a workman who was on a ladder doing some work on a house. This was the worst idea possible, as it made me sick. I found a bush next to some trees and spent the night there. I was so hungry that I felt like eating my genitals. I looked up at the branches of the tree and thought about the different knots you could make out of them. I came out from under the bush where I was sleeping and ate some blackberries. As the sun rose, I could see the sea and the seagulls soaring high in the sky. Again I saw the black helicopters way over my head, and I got scared, but my father's voice consoled me. I moved my legs, and they were stiff from not moving all night. I walked around Brighton and saw many signs in French and believed I was in France for a time because so many people were talking French. I was near where I had gone to art college, and I remembered the poverty I had seen in Peru and started crying.

I went and sat by the sea and the sun refreshed me. I saw a man with a strange tattoo and two boys get into the sea. I went into the water myself fully clothed and it was delicious. I got out and the sun dried my clothes. I walked on the beach and saw a circle of people and one person playing a bongo drum. I came up to them and started rapping. They passed a joint around but I didn't get any. Near Brighton pier there were a few people making a fire out of an old bicycle, and a black guy was fanning the flames with a rug. Eventually, the fire brigade came and put the fire out. I walked farther along the beach and saw a tunnel and walked into it. It was dark inside, and the path I was walking on was worn away to rubble. I kept bumping into people in the dark, and each time I did so, they sparked their lighters. Where the path ended, there was a staircase going down, but I was afraid of losing my footing and falling down, and I followed a rat to find my way out.

Then my luck changed. As I was walking beside the road, a van pulled up beside me and an Irish guy opened the door and asked me if I wanted a job. I said yes and hopped into the back of the van, which was empty aside from a few hammers. The men in the van bought me a hamburger at a shop, and I told them I was diagnosed with schizophrenia, but this didn't seem to bother them. They kept stopping the van to ask people if they wanted repairs done. I didn't know how I was going to help them, as I knew nothing about repair work. We got to a caravan park, and then we walked down the road to get a shower. It was a long way, but as we were walking along, I suddenly saw Peter go past on his bicycle. He stopped and came along with us until we finally reached a gym where there were showers, but it was closed and we had to walk back. We met up with other Irish travellers, who were all wearing the luminous yellow jackets that people wear who are working on roads. Peter and I got into another van with two Irishmen in it, but one of them started cursing him and he got out. It was two years before I saw him again. When he had gone, they took me to have a shower and a shave at a pub. I dowsed myself in cold water, but the plastic razor was blunt and could not cut through my shaggy beard.

We went back to the caravan, but they wouldn't let me sleep. They kept pointing to a place on the mattress and said, "Sleep there," but when I moved, they would say, "No, sleep over there." After a while I realised it was no use and got out of the caravan and went to another one. An Irishman and his son were there, and they gave me a beer. The man was chopping up onions with a sharp knife. "Do you believe in God?" I asked him. He said, "Definitely no." Finally, the Irishman who had brought me to the campsite came back and said, "You've got to go now," and I walked away into the night.

I went back to the beach and sat by the new pier and smoked my Lucky Strike cigarettes. I got into the sea and it wasn't that cold. I started speaking in verse, and I could hear the voices of my Irish friends in my head guiding me where to go. I picked some mussels

off a rock, intending to sell them. A lifeguard appeared and told me
to get out of the water, but I paid no attention. I was right under
the pier and another lifeguard dragged me out of the water. When
I reached the shore, two policemen asked me my name and later
took me to the police station. From there I was brought to a hospital
in Brighton, and then nurses came to bring me back to the ward in
Bethlem Royal.

By the time Henry reached Brighton, I was already looking for him.
I knew that I would worry so much about him while I was nominally
on holiday in Ireland that I would not be able to have a real rest, and
if I came back to England to look for him, it would at least give me
something to do. Jan and Alex might be able to have a proper holiday
knowing that I was doing all that could be done to find Henry.

I went first to Canterbury. I knew that the only way to find him
would be to keep in touch with his friends, whom he would probably
try to contact. I talked to Peter, who was torn between wanting to
help Henry and not wanting to give him away, but he knew that his
great friend could not survive for long on his own. He admitted that
he had accompanied Henry to Brighton before losing contact with
him.

I immediately went there after telling the police everything I
knew about Henry's whereabouts. Usually, I dealt with the Kent
police, but on this occasion he had disappeared in London, and his
case was being handled by the missing-persons unit of the Met-
ropolitan Police in south London. I put them in touch with Peter,
who gave them a detailed description of Henry's clothes: a white
T-shirt, beige trousers, and trainers. I knew that Henry's condition
would deteriorate each day because of lack of care and medication,

which he may have already stopped taking. This made it more likely that he would attract the attention of the police, but also more probable that he would do something leading to injury or death. I prepared a poster with Henry's photograph and description, which I was going to distribute around Brighton, where I had also given his picture to local newspapers. I was not very hopeful of finding him, but Peter, who was helping me, was bicycling to a shop to photocopy the poster about Henry when he unexpectedly saw him on a road in Brighton and briefly spoke to him. He told me Henry was with two men in Day-Glo yellow jackets who appeared to be Irish travellers in the building business. Peter had discovered that they came from a big encampment of travellers' caravans in the remnants of an aristocratic estate called Stanmer Park, now owned by Brighton Council. I went there with Peter, taking a taxi past a decayed gatehouse lodge into a field full of caravans. The travellers were friendly when I explained why I was there. One man said he was "ninety-nine percent certain" he had seen Henry with a group of travellers who were builders called Doran, but they had moved the previous day. People in other caravans said I should visit other "traveller" campsites, of which there seemed to be a depressingly large number on the south coast around Brighton. I was not too hopeful of finding Henry because Irish travellers are notoriously shy of the police and are likely to sympathise with any runaway.

I went back to the Old Ship Hotel, where I was staying once again, and where, later in the day, the police called me to say Henry had been found in the water by Brighton pier. My belief that his bizarre behaviour would draw attention to him turned out to be true, since he was spotted in the water fully clothed, speaking in verse, and picking shellfish off the rocks. I sat with him in Brighton Hospital, where the police had brought him and were guarding him until nurses from his hospital came to take him back. He was scratched, his hair was ragged, and he looked detached from the world around him, but at least he was alive. By now I had got the message that the National Psychosis Unit – though he was to stay there for five more months – was not going to help him make the breakthrough that would lead to his recovery.

CHAPTER SIXTEEN

Patrick

Henry's flight to Brighton and its predictably dismal conclusion were among my worst experiences during his long psychosis. There were to be other bad moments, but this was the last time I half expected a call from the police saying they had found his dead body. At the end of his eight-day disappearance, I thought of it gloomily as just one more heart-wrenching episode in the saga of his illness. I suspected it was all too likely that there would be others, especially as what happened underlined the failure of the National Psychosis Unit to bring about any improvement in his condition. Jan and I still hoped for the best from treatment at the Bethlem Royal, partly because there was no obvious alternative place for him to go. But we were also worried by rumours we heard from medical staff that Henry might be sent to some high-security psychiatric hospital far away in Northampton, in the depths of the English Midlands, where we would not be able to visit him regularly.

Once Henry recovered from his experiences in Brighton, I talked to him about not getting himself thrown out of the Bethlem Royal, and although he listened politely, I suspected my words were not having much impact. I even sent him a pleading letter in December 2006, promising that we would travel together when he got well. "If you do a few simple things," I wrote, "don't run away and take the medication (I know it does you good because I've seen you when you do take it and when you don't) – then we can do many wonderful things. We can go to Ireland. We can sail on the lakes. We can hire a barge and travel on the canals. And we could do all this in six months if you really want."

My plea had no effect. The psychosis ran too deep in his mind. Finally, after he broke out of Fitzmary 2 once more, the Bethlem Royal gave up, and in late January 2007 he was transferred, once again at a moment's notice, to a psychiatric hospital called Cygnet, in Beckton in the far east of London. It is not an alluring area. When Jan and I went to see Henry there for the first time, we found ourselves driving through the marshes north of the Thames, past a semi-derelict industrial landscape where the most visible feature is Britain's largest sewage works. We had been told that the landmark, which would tell us that we were close to Cygnet and should turn off the main road, was an artificial hill called the Beckton ski slopes, which has nothing to do with winter sports but once was part of a long-demolished gasworks. There may be attractive parts of Beckton, but if so, I never saw them. The district has a slightly sinister atmosphere, and a local taxi driver warned me that car theft was so common that insurance cost four times more than anywhere else in London. The hospital's grim surroundings were probably explained by the need to buy cheap land to build on. The hospital itself was private, though its patients were all paid for by the National Health Service. Henry had been sent there because Cygnet had a bed available, and health officials in east Kent said they had good experiences of the place. Its great advantage was that it had been recently built, and the design had taken into account the importance of hospitals which were truly secure but were not prisons. Cygnet's interior was fairly Spartan, and Henry's ward, called

Cob, could be reached only by passing through a series of locked doors. Cob had an open yard in the centre of the building, known as the garden, though there was more dismal grey cement than flowers and grass. The yard's existence was important because it was here that patients, including Henry, would smoke cigarettes, something they did obsessively. He would go there even in the rain to suck on a cigarette with a sort of desperate relish, as if it were an opium pipe.

The chief doctor was Humphrey Needham-Bennett, who seemed very much in control of the hospital and had a clear idea of what the priorities should be in treating Henry. These were to stop him running away – much more difficult for him to do at Cygnet than elsewhere – and to ensure that he took his clozapine, the only antipsychotic drug which appeared to do him any good. Measures to get him to take tablets can be easily stated, but to implement them effectively was tedious and immensely time-consuming. The pills had to be ground up and put in a glass of water, a fairly obvious precaution but one which was not done systematically before. A nurse also had to stay with him so he did not immediately make himself sick. He ran away twice by climbing on the roof of the hospital from the yard, but he did not try very hard to stop himself from being picked up and brought back. Despite these mishaps, Cygnet succeeded in increasing the amount of clozapine Henry received and in breaking the vicious circle of one step forward, two steps back, whereby Henry would make a slow partial recovery and then suffer an acute relapse.

By the end of 2007, the clozapine was having an effect, and Jan and I thought Henry was more engaged in the world and his thoughts and actions were less driven by hallucinations and voices. He appeared more rational, intelligent, and perceptive than we had seen him in five years, though we knew that this improvement would not last outside the hospital, since he openly admitted that he would stop taking his medication as soon as he could. We repeatedly asked for an experienced therapist who might at last persuade Henry he was ill and get him to take the medication voluntarily. At all the hospitals he was in, doctors always readily agreed to the usefulness of therapy as a general principle, but it never seemed to have a high priority, and there were frequent changes in the psychologists speaking to Henry. It was also true that much of the time he was probably too sick for a psychologist to do much good. Even if he had seen a therapist regularly, he distrusted medical and hospital staff to such a degree that he might never have taken their advice. A general failing on their part was that they never gave enough weight to the distress of patients who were being asked to take medication for the rest of their life which had serious side effects – Henry was half asleep much of the time and became fat – but did not cure the disorder. It is hardly surprising that studies of schizophrenia show that a fifth of inpatients and half of outpatients do not take the anti-psychotic drugs prescribed for them. When Henry finally did decide that he wanted to take his medication – as opposed to taking it under protest – as a defence against his polka-dot days, or brainstorms, it was conversations with his former yoga teacher which turned the scale.

Henry in the hospital corridor, 2008

As he got a little better, Henry started coming down to Canterbury in a car with two staff nurses for a few hours once every two
weeks. Jan and I individually, or together with Alex, would also take
him out in London, which at first was a nerve-racking and exhausting business. The first time he almost disappeared into a crowd when
we took him to a restaurant in Chinatown in central London; he was
brought back by Alex after a panic-stricken search. I realised that
future days out with Henry needed to be more carefully planned if
they were not going to end in disaster and we were all going to enjoy
them.

I looked for Beckton on a map in a food guide to London and discovered that there was a dispiriting lack of restaurants in and around
it. In time, however, I found places of interest we could get to fairly
quickly in a car. We visited the palaces and parks on the other side
of the Thames at Greenwich; country churches with fading medieval wall paintings in Essex; and pubs serving good food in ancient
hamlets in West Kent. Eating in pubs was a little testing for Henry
because his doctors did not allow him to drink alcohol, less because
of the damage it would do to him – he was never a big drinker –
than because of a general ban on alcohol at Cygnet, where several
of the patients were reformed alcoholics. Once we went to visit the
village of Tudeley in West Kent, where, in the small and otherwise
undistinguished local church, the windows are all by Marc Chagall,
their glass bright with wonderful swirling blues in which float angels,
donkeys, and fish. The local landowner's daughter was drowned
in 1961 while boating off Rye on the south coast (not so far from
where Henry had almost died at Newhaven), and Chagall was hired
to design memorial windows. In one of them, the dead girl is shown
bathed in blue as she ascends a ladder to heaven. Henry was at first
uninterested but gradually became fascinated by the other windows,
where blue is replaced by dancing yellows and whites.

Henry was essentially a city person, and we used to go to Brick Lane in the East End, which is overlooked by the tall buildings of the City next door. Famous for its Bengali restaurants, Brick Lane turned out to be something of a tourist trap, selling inferior South Asian food at excessive prices. But Henry and I found nearby a large student café housed in the remains of an old brewery where the customers were his age and not too alarmed by his habit of starting conversations with total strangers when they sat at our table. Being reserved myself and inhibited in talking to strangers, I was initially embarrassed, but most people suddenly addressed by Henry were pleased to talk, and some, who at first seemed dull, described lives that were full of interest and strange turns. I remember my father telling me that he never found anybody truly boring, and in conversation with him, people I dismissed as dreary would begin to sparkle and reveal startling facts about themselves or tell funny stories. Henry would do the same thing. Once he fell into conversation with a man in a wheelchair who turned out to be a Serb from Belgrade who had started a successful graphic design company despite being handicapped from birth by stunted hands and legs. Having listened attentively to Henry's account of his time in mental hospitals, the Serb refreshingly concluded that worse things happened to people and it would not be too difficult for Henry to put his life back on track.

I thought that for variety, we should visit as many different parts of London as we could. Henry showed knowledge of places where the homeless, among whom he had sought refuge during his escapes, liked to gather. He could quickly get on terms with them because, despite my urgings, he was usually dressed like a vagrant, wearing a grubby shirt or T-shirt, jeans or tracksuit bottoms, and battered trainers, and with his hair all awry. It was as if he saw his dishevelled appearance as essential to his identification with the poor and outcast. He refused to smarten up his appearance and dress even when making one of his many failed appeals to the tribunal, which decided whether he should be detained under the Mental Health Act. Vainly urged by sympathetic nurses to comb his hair and change into clean clothes to help persuade the tribunal that he was well enough to resume normal life, he stuck to his torn shirt and dirty trousers.

Sitting with Henry in student cafés in Brick Lane or more expensive ones in Covent Garden, I thought about the ways his mental illness had affected him and our family over the previous seven years. By this time, in the first half of 2008, when he was twenty-six years old, he was obviously better than he had been, but then, at his worst, he had been very bad indeed; the improvement was comparative. Often he would be apathetic and dozy, particularly for the first hour after he had left Beckton, but then he would start to perk up, speaking intelligently and coherently and showing curiosity about the world around him. But just as I would be thinking optimistically how sane he sounded, he would say something that showed that he did not distinguish between what was real and the world of his imagination. There was, for instance, a sordid and evil-smelling smoking room in the hospital at Cygnet that had a machine on the wall where patients lit their cigarettes by pressing a green button. The purpose was to keep matches and lighters out of their hands. Henry said he believed in all seriousness that there was a green dragon in a huge cavern under the hospital which was woken by the button and breathed fire on a metal object, which transmitted heat to the surface, where it ignited the patients' cigarettes.

Compulsions, which might be very ordinary but were sometimes very strange, as well as obsessive interests, would frequently determine what Henry did or said. He spent a lot of his waking life thinking about where he could get his next cigarette and where he could smoke it. I had once been a chain-smoker myself, but I had never seen an addiction so deep. There were topics which absorbed him, as if his mind were caught in a rut. These included an obsessive interest in the Haitian-American graffiti artist Basquiat, his relationship with the girl Elisa whom he had known briefly in Brighton, and his devotion to rap, music I never liked and which often seemed to me to be self-indulgent doggerel. I tried not to praise Henry's paintings or raps unless I really thought they were good, because to do anything else would be to treat him like a child. I did not want to reinforce the infantilisation stemming from his long years in institutions. Much of the time Henry was warm, affectionate, and sociable, but I could also see a streak of childlike egotism. While he often felt excessive and unnecessary guilt, he showed no guilt at all about the frantic anxiety he caused Jan, Alex, and me whenever he ran away.

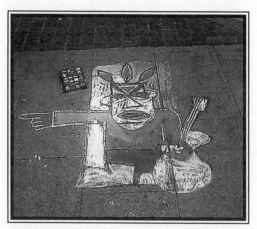

Henry's pavement chalk drawing of a demon in
memory of a street musician who died from
heroin in 2009

By the time Henry began to show slow but sustained signs of improvement from late 2007 on, Jan and I had long experience of his psychoses. We had come through repeated crises surprisingly well because we supported each other and never seriously disagreed about what to do for him. In coping with the seemingly endless crises, we had the advantage of large and supportive families. Jan had her sisters Teresa and Catherine, and I had my brothers Alexander and Andrew, both of whom lived in the US but were available on the phone. We had more nieces than nephews, and they came to see Henry in different hospitals. Meriel, Teresa's daughter, flew from Barcelona when she first heard that he was ill. Daisy, Alexander's daughter, went to see him often and talked to him on the phone. I thought that for a single parent or parents without resources, caring for a schizophrenic would be an unsustainable nightmare. Rather unexpectedly, our careers did not suffer very much while Henry was in the hospital, probably because in my case, having to survive in Baghdad during the war – I had returned to *The Independent* as a correspondent – was at least a diversion from the strain of dealing with his problems.

The member of the family worst affected by what happened to Henry was neither Jan nor me but his brother, Alex, who was young and vulnerable. He was understandably worried about his brother, to whom he had been close. But he also found that his parents' concerns were nearly all about Henry when he himself was feeling very unhappy at school and in need of support. For him, the crisis could not have come at a worse time. Age fourteen when Henry had his first breakdown, Alex was already having problems at King's School, which he had entered as top scholar, a status that was the equivalent of winning a valuable scholarship, since it cut his school fees in half. Once in the school, he felt that he was not measuring up to his and his teachers' expectations that he would immediately demonstrate his high mathematical ability, and this depressed him. At first Alex says he did not quite grasp what was happening to Henry in his last weeks as a student in Brighton, but he soon found he could no longer communicate with him. Alex was only fifteen when Henry was sectioned, and he had an appalling experience, described earlier by both brothers, when Henry had a spectacular breakdown as Alex was escorting him back to St Martin's hospital in 2003. Henry has since explained that was the first of his polka-dot days. With heroic resolution Alex coaxed Henry, naked and sobbing with fear from his delusions, to get dressed and return to the hospital.

For a time Alex felt weighed down by anxiety over Henry's frequent disappearances and, after producing stellar exam results for years, started missing lessons at school. He dutifully visited his brother in the hospital, but these visits were often difficult, because Henry would try to assert primacy as the elder brother. Alex could never quite come to terms with the schizophrenia, partly because he felt Henry's view of the world was fundamentally wrong. The world of dreams – or rather, the mixture of real and imaginary which so often possessed Henry's mind – was in direct contrast to Alex's concrete and rational approach to life. Alex wanted to do everything to help his elder brother but felt anger towards Henry for monopolising his parents' attention when he himself desperately needed attention and support. He also silently resented the fact that Henry never took responsibility for anything he did, such as running away, though his actions had a devastating effect on the rest of his family. What made it worse for Alex was that, although Henry adored his brother, he could also be inconsiderate and rude to him and to Jan in a way that he never was to me. Once Alex spent an entire day travelling to and from Beckton – the hospital was difficult to get to directly by train from Canterbury – only to have Henry swear continuously at him for not bringing cigarettes. Jan and I realised that Alex might feel neglected, and we did what we could to support him. But inevitably, we had no choice but to give most of our attention to Henry when we thought his life was in danger.

"Do you think I am a failure, Dad?" Henry used to ask me sadly. I would reply truthfully that life had dealt him a tough hand, for reasons that were absolutely not his fault. But as his lucidity increased, I asked myself how he could live happily in the future. His life had been deep frozen over seven years while he was in different hospitals, and more time would pass before he would be able to survive outside. Many of his friends in Canterbury and elsewhere had moved on since he knew them: they had gone to university, got jobs, married, and had children. Those whom he still saw often took drugs or had mental health problems of their own. I knew that Henry was downcast by a sense that life was passing him by, that he was in his late twenties and his future prospects were bleak.

As Henry's mental condition improved, in late 2007 I began to cast around for a project that I could help him carry out. I came to realise that his greatest disadvantage in life might be turned into an asset: he knew everything about what it is like to have a mental illness and to live in mental hospitals for years. My profession was writing, and I had come to know a great deal about schizophrenia from the outside. Why not combine these strengths and write about his schizophrenia from his and my points of view? I also thought that writing about his disorder might make it easier for Henry to admit that he had an illness and open the door for him to take his medication voluntarily. I suspected he did not want to confess to being mentally ill – and who does? – because to do so was humiliating and discredited his whole view of himself and the world. I recalled that when he and I were walking around Brighton after his first breakdown, he had been embarrassed when I spoke too loudly in a restaurant about his being in the Priory and taking the anti-psychotic drug olanzapine. If, instead of telling people he was in a mental hospital, he could say he was writing a book about his experiences, it would be good for his morale and self-confidence.

By the summer of 2008, I felt Henry was well enough for us to go ahead with our project. His doctors agreed. At first he was shy about writing, and I brought him a copy of Günter Grass's *The Tin Drum*, the opening words of which famously read "Granted: I am an inmate of a mental hospital . . ." Then Henry began to write in his beautifully distinct handwriting, so much clearer than Jan's or my own, describing what had happened to him. I thought it would be best to have a trial run of our twin narratives in a newspaper. Our article appeared in September 2008 in a supplement of *The Independent* and was highly praised. Encouraged by the reception, we started work on the book in the spring of 2009. At this stage, Henry's mental balance was improving, and working on the book appeared to give him a sense of purpose and accomplishment.

For months Jan and I pressed Dr Needham-Bennett to plan for Henry to go somewhere he would have more freedom in recognition of his improvement and because we thought he would be happier there. It would be a momentous step for him since he had spent all of the previous five years in mental hospitals. The staff at Beckton was cautious about him leaving permanently because, while Henry was a lot better, there were moments – which he said happened about once a week and lasted several hours – when he was racked by acute mental distress. As early as late 2007, he had begun to say grudgingly that his medication helped prevent these agonies. Two years later, Henry was spending every weekend in Canterbury and two days a week at a step-down facility, really a well-staffed rehabilitation unit, which was part of the Cygnet hospital group in Lewisham in southeast London.

The facility in Lewisham was in a large converted house opposite a park in an inner London suburb and felt more like a normal place to live than the prison-hospital atmosphere of the hospital in Beckton. It was also heavily staffed and geared towards helping patients learn to live outside an institutional framework. But it was not a halfway house, such as the one in Ramsgate where Henry had spent a disastrous few months in 2003, and which was effectively a hostel for recovering mental patients. That would be too much of a jump for Henry after his long confinement during which everything was done for him.

In October 2009 Henry moved to Lewisham full-time, and his mood became more optimistic and relaxed. He still looked like a tramp, though a rather better dressed one than a year earlier, and because we are almost exactly the same size, he was always borrowing my clothes and frequently failing to return them. I told him that handing over my jackets, trousers, and jerseys to him was like sending troops over the top in World War I. While an early sign of his illness had been when Jan and Alex found that he had dismembered his mobile phone, now, in early 2010, he is using a mobile and a laptop and complaining vigourously when they do not work. He says he still feels a strong impulse to run away, but he successfully resists it and has not done so in over two years.

Henry singing with a street musician in London, 2008

The psychosis has not disappeared. One evening in January 2010, I arrived at the house in Lewisham to take Henry out to supper. I was looking forward to it because he had become much more alert and able to enjoy himself, but I found him incoherent, shaking with fear, and in the midst of one of his brainstorms. We decided it was best if he lay down, and I sat beside his bed for an hour until he recovered. Crucially, he has decided that the cocktail of drugs he takes – though he strongly resents their side effects – does help him combat his polka-dot days. I do not wholly understand how he reached this decision, and he still expresses misgivings, but he no longer appears to see medication as the instrument of other people trying to control his life. He has also forsworn marijuana, though he still feels strongly drawn to it. I hope all this will last. I recognise that we, as a family, will always have to cope with the consequences of his schizophrenia. But that, after all, is what families are for. In the face of his torments, Henry has been baffled but also brave in withstanding all the miseries so unjustly inflicted on him. I wonder about his future, but it is too early to make concrete plans. At this stage, it is enough for me that Henry, now twenty-eight, has survived and has a chance to lead a happy life.

I have learned a lot about schizophrenia since the first terrifying days when I saw Henry in Brighton after he nearly drowned in the English Channel, and I am no longer as ignorant and frightened of it as I once was. Even at his most insane, Henry never entirely lost his grip on reality, so I no longer think of people going on a one-way journey from complete sanity to total madness. Writing about his own state of mind after he had admitted himself to a mental hospital in the South of France in 1889, Vincent van Gogh exactly describes the importance of this perception: "Although there are a few people here who are seriously ill, the fear, the horror that I had of madness before has already been greatly softened." To his surprise, he found that his fellow patients, though they might howl and shout in the night, were friendly, considerate, helpful to him and to one another, and had lost nothing of their humanity.

At first I looked on Henry's schizophrenia as a disease which either would or would not be cured. But everything to do with Henry's illness appears more fluid and less predictable to me now than it once did. Today I see it more as a mental disorder, which is very difficult to eliminate but can perhaps be confined to a corner of Henry's mind and will no longer be the driving force in his personality and his actions that it once was.

Henry increasingly recognises the existence of his illness and is more combative towards it. "I began to have the polka dots earlier today," he phoned me recently to say, "but I dealt with them."

"You defeated them?"

"Yes, I defeated them," he replied with some relish.

His voices and visions may still call to him, but they are no longer sure of an answer.

CHAPTER SEVENTEEN
Henry

During the past seven years, I have been in a mental hospital, and during those seven years I have escaped over thirty times. I felt a call from the natural world to run away from where I was incarcerated. The last time I ran away was almost two years ago. I heard a voice in my head that spoke to me in rhyme. It told me to run away, and sometimes it told me to remove my clothes and go into the forest, and when I did so, the forest would come alive and speak to me. The tree roots would move at the touch of my finger, and I would see images in my mind as if I were watching television.

I arrived at Cygnet after I had run away from the Bethlem Royal for about the sixth consecutive time. The staff from Beckton came to pick me up and drove me to a hospital in the middle of a housing estate in east London. When I arrived, it still had a smoking room, something that has been banned; now, if you want to smoke, you have to stand outside. The smoking room in Beckton had metal benches and a big square table in the middle of the room with one window looking out at some pine trees. I was in Cob ward, which was an all-male unit, and the people when I first arrived were all very tough. Many of them had been in prison, and at first I was bullied a bit. One patient was called George and had his daughter's name, Kayleigh, tattooed on his neck. He asked if I wanted to join the extreme right-wing British National Party, and I said no. Later, he made me sit under a tree at the end of the courtyard because he found out I was partly Jewish. It was the only tree in the hospital complex, and later, it was dug up and removed. There was another guy in the ward with a tattoo of a swastika on his chest. I remember him smuggling in some alcohol. The courtyard looked much as I imagined one in a prison might. I suggested that they get a basketball hoop, and after six months they did.

After a few months a couple of people I had known from Canterbury turned up. There was Jason, who was a bit younger than me and had tattoos in a Celtic design which he had done himself when he was in prison. Another friend I saw was Clive, who was black and from Jamaica and endlessly smoked roll-ups. We used to talk about music: he said you couldn't mix acid jazz with hip-hop. Sometimes I would play chess, and once I burned myself on my left forearm with a cigarette because I lost. It was either that or breaking up my guitar. I wrote a rap about "boredom and rage in a cage." Life in a locked ward is miserably boring, and it is instant bliss running away, but a dash for freedom usually lasts only a few days, until I am picked up by the police.

I escaped twice from Beckton the first year I was there. The walls of the garden had what looked like big black rolling pins attached to the top to stop people from getting on top of the wall and then onto the roof. I was less plump in those days – since then the medication they give me has made me fat – and I was able to climb onto the roof and make the long jump down on the outside of the hospital. I got on a train to Charing Cross and later got lost on Oxford Street but made my way to Waterloo Station. I went to a pub nearby, and somebody bought me a drink. As I was walking back to the station, my world suddenly collapsed and I felt I was going to die. I walked along the embankment of the Thames feeling terrible and fighting the urge to jump in. I listened to the loud tolling of Big Ben and thought it was tolling the end of my existence. I saw some policewomen coming towards me, and I stopped them and told them I had run away from a hospital. They took me back to the clinic.

The last time I absconded, I hurt my foot jumping down from the outside wall of the hospital. I went to Brighton by train, as I had done from Bethlem Royal a year earlier, but unfortunately, once there I was stupid enough to beg a spliff off two men and tell them my full story. This was that I had written a suicide letter and then ripped it up and decided to go to Brighton. They called the police, and I spent the night in a police cell. Back at Cygnet, they decided it was too risky to let me into the yard, and a man came to put new locks on the doors.

Inside the hospital, life was lonely and the place looked like a semi-open prison. Each day was the same: I would mix with other patients and get my medication. This ritual was played out twice a day. The nurse ground up the clozapine tablets and added water so I couldn't spit them out. We had gym twice a week. I painted pictures and sometimes thought it would be good to go back to art college. I slept during the day and stayed up most of the night. I coped with boredom by smoking and playing my guitar. I would have liked to go to live music events, chilling with my friends, but then I looked at the big metal grilles on the windows and remembered I was incarcerated. At one point I thought my room was being bugged, so I got on top of the cupboard and dismantled a black box on the wall just above it. At another, I thought that an evil spirit had got into the building. My old babysitter David Mitchell, now a famous novelist, had written a book about a spirit which could only appear in this world as a shadow. I thought he was writing about a demon that appeared in sunlight, while most demons appeared only at night. I thought George, the patient who bullied me and supported the BNP, was being controlled by a solar demon because the demon wanted the gold ring on his finger. I told the staff about this, but they did not seem very worried.

By my second year at Beckton in 2008, I had been sectioned about eleven times. "I can hear what you are saying," said the psychiatrist as, with the stroke of a pen, he renewed my section over my protests. I wondered if he realised what power he had in that pen. When it comes to being sectioned, what a professional psychiatrist says carries a lot of weight compared to that of somebody who has been diagnosed as a schizophrenic. He said he believed I was a risk to myself because I used to swim in rivers and lakes.

Once I was so angry at this that I planned revenge on a psychiatrist. I had seen an enormous spider in the hospital garden and knew the spider lived in a corner between a windowpane and a wall. I thought I would capture the spider and let it loose near the psychiatrist so it would bite him. I got a cup and urinated on the spiderweb, and the spider started to run away. I caught it successfully in the cup, but it was facedown on the wall and I did not have a card to put over the face of the cup. A credit card would have been useful. I tried to make do with a packet of Marlboro cigarettes, but the spider got away and I did not fancy my chances of recapturing it in the dark. A few days later, I saw the same spider in the garden, but it was looking even bigger and much more menacing. It was twice its previous size and I thought that the saying that what doesn't kill you makes you stronger is as true of spiders as it is of humans. But I thought also that the poor psychiatrist did not deserve to be attacked by a giant spider, so I let it go.

These days I'm in a step-down or rehabilitation unit in Lewisham. My attitude to medication has changed a little. I take the tablets and don't think they do me any harm. But every now and again I think I should have escaped and not agreed to take my medication. I am still not sure I am mentally ill. It is certain that I do hear voices and that some people do not hear voices. I remember when I didn't. Now I hear voices inside my head, so they are like external thoughts.

I am allowed out for three hours a day of unescorted leave. I usually go to a café called Kem's Caf. I sit in the back, chain-smoking cigarettes, drinking cappuccinos, and talking to customers. I go to meetings with other patients about social skills, art, and computers, and I am doing a series of paintings. On weekends I go back to Canterbury and see my mother, father, and brother at our family home. Lewisham is a big transition from Beckton, which always felt a bit like a jail. I don't run away anymore, though the temptation is incessant. I get the daemons or polka dots, which feel like a bad trip, about once a week, but they last less time than they used to, sometimes as little as two hours. When this happens, I just go to my bed and try and sleep them off. This usually works. I am a firm believer in Christ now. He gives me strength. When things get bad, I sometimes read my Bible and find comfort in that. The staff is nice in Lewisham, and the food is moderately good. There is a chef there with an extraordinarily bad temper if you are late for your food, which I mostly am. We go swimming once a week. I haven't smoked marijuana in about six months and feel a bit the better for it. Paranoia sets in when you smoke dope. You keep thinking that they will screen you for drugs. Sometimes when it is night and I want to go for a stroll and feel the night air, I wish I were free. I read my raps at poetry events in cafés, and when this goes well, I feel good and like I'm heading in the right direction. I smoke too much and am fearful that I use my cigarette smoking as a crutch when life becomes difficult.

My love life is nowhere. I spend the nights reading in the bath. Books, I devour them. It seems ironic, but now any hint of the cold gives me the shivers and I go inside, yet once I survived sitting naked in snowdrifts. I am in London, where the trees always told me to go. I love the big red buses, all the different colours and different people from all over the world. I was born in London, and maybe that is why I feel so much at home there. I see the psychiatrist every Monday. I am still on section, which means that everything I do is at the doctor's discretion. The psychiatrist seems nice and listens to what I have to say, but he has his own agenda. He does not remove my sectioning, telling me that it is necessary to keep tabs on my progress in the hospital. I get the impression that if Socrates himself wrote my appeal against being sectioned, it would still be turned down by the doctor. During my years in mental hospitals, I have met a lot of psychiatrists, and none of them wants to take risks. Maybe they feel their jobs are on the line and are scared that I will run under a bus if I am free.

It has been a very long road for me, but I think I'm entering the final straight. There is a tree I sit under in the garden in Lewisham which speaks to me and gives me hope.

ACKNOWLEDGMENTS

I would like to thank Colin Robinson for originally commissioning the book and our editor, Samantha Martin, who provided crucial help in shaping the text and keeping Henry and me focussed while we were writing it. Her perceptive comments and tactful criticism played an essential part in producing each chapter.

The sources for the book are primarily the memories of Henry, Jan, Alex, and me. These are supplemented by Jan's diary excerpt and by the many letters that Jan wrote to doctors about Henry during his illness and a smaller number of letters I wrote.

I am grateful to Jan for closely reading everything which Henry and I produced and offering valuable commentary and suggestions. Thanks are due to Alex, who read the manuscript and wrote a description of how events had affected him. I was also helped by my brothers, Alexander and Andrew Cockburn, reading the book during different stages of its production and offering useful encouragement and advice.

The doctors and nurses who treated Henry and spoke to his anxious parents over the years are too numerous to be thanked individually, but I owe heartfelt thanks to them all – and to the many friends and relatives who visited Henry in the hospital and kept in touch even at the grimmest moments of his disorder.

Notes

Chapter Eight

93   "In February 2001, a year before . . ." E-mails from Desmond
      King, September 29 and 30, 2009. Private conversations with King.

94   "Of young Americans diagnosed with schizophrenia . . ."
      Schizophrenia Facts and Statistics, http://www.schizophrenia
      .com/szfacts.htm.

95   "'While schizophrenia is by no means . . .'" Philip M. Boffey,
      "Schizophrenia: Insights Fail to Halt Rising Toll," *The New
      York Times*, March 16, 1986.

95   "Of the six hundred thousand homeless living rough . . ."
      Schizophrenia.com.

96   "He told me, however, that a full and accurate account . . ."
      David Reed, *Anna* (London, Penguin Books, 1977), passim.

97   "Dr John A. Talbott, a former president . . ." Boffey,
      "Schizophrenia."

98   "In the UK, more than one in three people . . ." BBC, August
      9, 2009. The YouGov poll was commissioned by Time to
      Change.

99   "The long-term effectiveness of any kind of medication
        . . ." Sophia Frangou and Robin M. Murray, *Schizophrenia*
        (London, Martin Dunitz, 2000), p. 57.

99   "Possibly because of frustration by the lack of real progress
        . . ." Richard P. Bentall, *Madness Explained: Psychosis and
        Human Nature* (London, Allen Lane, 2003), p. 156.

101   "The conventional approach to understanding madness . . ."
        Bentall, *Madness Explained*.

102   "The highly authoritative manual . . ." Schizophrenia
        Research Forum interview with Robin Murray, October
        18, 2005, http://www.schizophreniaforum.org/for/int/
        Murray/murray.asp.

108   "It is even possible for two people to be diagnosed . . ."
        Richard Bentall, "Diagnoses Are Psychiatry's Star Signs.
        Let's Listen More and Drug People Less," *The Guardian*,
        September 1, 2009.

CHAPTER NINE

109   "Studies show that a child . . ." Frangou and Murray,
        Schizophrenia, p. 18.

110   "In any case, the process by which the disorder is transmitted"
        David G. Kingdon and Douglas Turkington, *Cognitive
        Therapy of Schizophrenia* (New York and London, Guilford
        Press, 2005), p. 5.

111   "When Hugh was a sixteen-year-old schoolboy . . ."
        Hugh Montefiore, *Oh God, What Next?: An Autobiography*
        (London, Hodder & Stoughton, 1995), p. 2.

114   "One of the world's greatest experts on cannabis . . ." Dr
        Thomas Stuttaford, "Cannabis: It's Time for a Rethink,"
        The Times, December 19, 2005.

117   "Evelyn Waugh, one of the great . . ." Evelyn Waugh,

The Ordeal of Gilbert Pinfold (London, Chapman & Hall, 1957), passim. For a full account of Waugh's breakdown, see Christopher Sykes, *Evelyn Waugh* (London, Collins, 1975), pp. 359–78.

CHAPTER TWELVE

157   "In 1 per cent of cases..." Frangou and Murray, *Schizophrenia*, p. 41.

167   "By the autumn of 2005 . . ." The National Psychosis Unit is at Bethlem Royal Hospital in Beckenham, which in turn is part of the South London and Maudsley National Health Service Trust. Confusingly, the hospital Henry was in is often referred to as the Maudsley.

CHAPTER FOURTEEN

184   "Health experts increasingly see . . ." Oliver Sacks, "The Lost Virtues of the Asylum," *The New York Review of Books*, September 24, 2009.

185   "In reality, British Health Minister John Hutton..." "Mentally Ill Face Compulsory Treatment," BBC, November 16, 1999, http://news.bbc.co.uk.1/hi//health/521485.stm.

185   "Between the 1950s and today . . ." Amy Nelmes, "Shocking Number of Murders Committed by Mental Patients," *The People*, June 14, 2009.

185   "In the US the number of beds available . . ." Treatment Advocacy Center, "The Shortage of Public Hospital Beds for Mentally Ill Persons," Arlington, Virginia, 2008.

186   "The British detective-story writer..." P. D. James, *Time to Be in Earnest: A Fragment of Autobiography* (London, Faber & Faber, 1999), pp. 177–80.

188   "There are at least fifty such . . ." BBC, March 2, 2010.

189   "A schizophrenic patient is a hundred times . . ." Frangou and
       Murray, *Schizophrenia*, pp. 67–69.

Chapter Sixteen

214   "Writing about his own state of mind . . ." *Vincent van Gogh:*
       The Letters, Volume 5 (London and New York, Thames &
       Hudson, 2009), pp. 12–23.

INDEX

About the Authors

Patrick Cockburn is the Iraq correspondent for *The Independent* in London. He has received the Martha Gellhorn Prize for war reporting, the James Cameron Award, and the Orwell Prize for journalism. He is the author of *Muqtada al-Sadr*, about war and rebellion in Iraq; *The Occupation* (short-listed for a National Book Critics Circle Award in 2007); *The Broken Boy*, a memoir; and, with Andrew Cockburn, *Out of the Ashes: The Resurrection of Saddam Hussein*.

Henry Cockburn was born in London and raised in Canterbury, where he attended King's School and received several awards for his artwork. In 2002, during his first year at Brighton Art College, he was diagnosed with schizophrenia. He currently resides at a rehabilitation centre in London.